What Your Colleagues Are Saying...

As our world changes, we must also change the way we think about leading, teaching, and learning. *7 Mindshifts for School Leaders* offers practical strategies for how to make meaningful change to positively impact school communities for the better. This is a must-read book for all school leaders.

Starr Sackstein
Author and COO of Mastery Portfolio, LLC
Oceanside, NY

7 Mindshifts for School Leaders is a stand-out game-changer! Hamilton, Jones, and Vari offer real-time ideas and examples to support you with current leadership strategies. They provide a blueprint for implementing effective change to bolster student achievement.

Matthew X. Joseph
CEO X-Factor EDU
Boston, MA

Hamilton, Jones, and Vari empower school leaders to craft new solutions for age-old problems. This framework is an inspiring pathway and highly doable. Each new lens offered is complemented with a plethora of relatable examples, strategies, and resources.

Aubrey Patterson
CEO and Founding Partner of Warm Demanders Inc.
Edmonton, Alberta, Canada

The seven mindshifts shared by Hamilton, Jones, and Vari give current and upcoming school leaders a fresh way to think about the unique problems their schools are facing. The easy-to-read format offers the models and mindshifts school leaders need to develop solutions to issues such as classroom management, achievement gaps, teacher retention, and more. It is a must-read for all leaders.

Nathan Maynard
Author/Coach/Founder of the Restorative Group
Indianapolis, IN

In *7 Mindshifts for School Leaders,* Hamilton, Jones, and Vari lay the foundation for how leaders of the next generation will need to think differently to effect change and impact our schools. Reading this book is the first step in creating the mindshifts needed to fight decades-old battles in education. Let's start the revolution!

Salome Thomas-EL
Award-Winning Principal, Speaker, and Author
Wilmington, DE

I love a book that is unabashedly deep. *7 Mindshifts* is brimming with new insights and ideas for action. Each of the mindshifts is unique and rich with analysis and directional solutions. Take time with each mindshift. Savor it in its own right. Each one is a change theory on its own. The seven together cross-cut and stimulate more ideas about how we might find new ways to think about old problems in education.

Michael Fullan
Professor Emeritus, OISE/University of Toronto
Toronto, Ontario, Canada

We exponentially increase our chances of solving the vast challenges facing education when we adopt a crisis mindset. Enough with planning and strategizing! *7 Mindshifts for School Leaders* is an all hands on deck call to action.

Daniel Bauer
Chief Ruckus Maker, Better Leaders Better Schools
Syracuse, NY

Hamilton, Jones, and Vari redefine what we mean by crisis and explain the mindshifts needed for effective school leadership. Their ambition is no less than to solve persistent, fundamental problems in education. This book should sit on school leaders' desks with many dog-eared pages and highlighted sections. It leads educators to the right place to start and the methods to sustain the positive changes all students desperately need.

S. David Brazer
Brazer Education Consulting
Petaluma, CA

7 Mindshifts for School Leaders

Finding New Ways to Think About Old Problems

Connie Hamilton
Joseph Jones
T.J. Vari

Foreword by Joe Sanfelippo

For information:

Corwin
A SAGE Company
2455 Teller Road
Thousand Oaks, California 91320
(800) 233-9936
www.corwin.com

SAGE Publications Ltd.
1 Oliver's Yard
55 City Road
London, EC1Y 1SP
United Kingdom

SAGE Publications India Pvt. Ltd.
B 1/I 1 Mohan Cooperative
Industrial Area
Mathura Road, New Delhi 110 044
India

SAGE Publications Asia-Pacific
Pte. Ltd.
18 Cross Street #10-10/11/12
China Square Central
Singapore 048423

President: Mike Soules
Vice President and Editorial Director: Monica Eckman
Senior Acquisitions Editor: Tanya Ghans
Content Development Manager: Desirée A. Bartlett
Editorial Assistant: Nyle De Leon
Production Editor: Vijayakumar
Copy Editor: Christobel Colleen Hopman
Typesetter: TNQ Technologies
Proofreader: Benny Willy Stephen
Indexer: TNQ Technologies
Cover Designer: Gail Buschman
Marketing Manager: Morgan Fox
Cover Art: Paul Hamilton III

Printed in Canada

Library of Congress Cataloging-in-Publication Data

Names: Hamilton, Connie, author. | Jones, Joseph, author. | Vari, T.J., author.

Title: 7 mindshifts for school leaders : finding new ways to think about old problems / Connie Hamilton, Joseph Jones, T.J. Vari.

Other titles: Seven mindshifts for school leaders Description: Thousand Oaks, California : Corwin Press, [2023] | Includes bibliographical references and index.

Identifiers: LCCN 2022040443 | ISBN 9781071871065 (paperback) | ISBN 9781071871096 (adobe pdf) | ISBN 9781071871072 (epub) | ISBN 9781071871089 (epub)

Subjects: LCSH: Educational leadership–Psychological aspects. | School management and organization. | Problem solving. | Educational change.

Classification: LCC LB2806 .H326 2023 | DDC 371.2–dc23/eng/20220902

LC record available at https://lccn.loc.gov/2022040443

This book is printed on acid-free paper.

22 23 24 25 26 10 9 8 7 6 5 4 3 2 1

CONTENTS

FOREWORD

By Joe Sanfelippo

"You have the build for running. You should be a runner." That comment made me laugh so hard that I was thankful I hadn't just taken a sip of water, or I would have spit it out. My friend, Tony, then went into a monologue on the benefits of running. The only time I had ever thought of running was during a bad dream in which I was being chased by a wild animal. But Tony was so convincing that the next day I went out and bought a brand-new pair of shoes, new ear buds, and one of those things runners use to attach phones to their arms. In less than 24 hours, I had gone from never running to setting a goal to be a marathon runner. I woke up the following day to begin "marathon training." The Couch to 5K app, apparently knowing more than I do about running, indicated that I only needed to run for 7 minutes. Clearly the app didn't understand that I was a marathoner. I decided instead to run until I was tired. Afterward, I felt really good. I even got a taste of what Tony called "the runner's high."

On my way to work, I felt amazing. I drank a lot of water because us runners, we hydrate. I stretched in the hallways so I could tell people I was stretching from my run. That day, I was a runner and I saw marathons in my future. The next morning, however, I couldn't feel my legs. I started to ratio-nalize everything in my world. I thought, *I am going to be traveling next week. I don't know if my shoes are going to fit in my bag. I don't even know if they have roads where I am going. I'll just wait until I get back to start my running career.* That week turned into months and months turned into years. I have the most expensive lawn mowing shoes in the county and I have never even run a 5K, let alone a marathon.

I had the shoes, the app, the ear buds, the thing on the arm. What I didn't have were the two things that I needed to make it work: persistence and the immediacy to change my behavior. Had I been chased by a wild animal I wouldn't have had the chance to rationalize or delay, I would have run and continued running because survival is worth the time and effort.

This same mindset applies to our roles as leaders in education. When we fail to see the urgency of issues, or rely on things instead of our own commitment, our practice remains the same and our problems persist. The pandemic was our wild animal. It removed the option to delay. We had to do *something* and do it quickly. Schools across the country were able to accomplish in weeks that had previously taken years. The crisis mindset required us to take immediate action and out of those efforts came incredible benefits to students and families. We now have systems that give us the ability to connect from anywhere, the aligning of curriculum because we weren't afforded the amount of time we had in the past, and new ways to demonstrate because we were in different places. We now need to ask ourselves if we can use that mindshift to move faster and provide better opportunities for those we serve.

7 Mindshifts for School Leaders does just that. Connie, T.J., and Joe have done an amazing job of breaking down how school leaders can use the crisis mindset of the pandemic to take on the problems that have plagued us for decades. Each chapter offers school leaders a new way of thinking that will help them find solutions to persistent problems. The authors relate success stories from outside of education to show how those mindshifts and strategies can be used as game changers in education. Technical tips such as the Crisis Filter tool in Chapter 1 will help you determine whether a problem should be treated as a crisis. The end of chapter reflection questions will not only help you and your team delve into thoughtful analysis regarding the particular challenges in your school, they also prompt readers to take immediate action in their own settings.

The strategies in this book are practical, but more importantly, you will see yourself and your team in the examples. That connection sets this book apart and will set your group apart from those who aren't willing make the mindshifts necessary to provide better opportunities for those we serve. As you read this book, prepare to face your own wild animals and be challenged, but also supported, in a way that will change the way you lead.

Joe Sanfelippo is the superintendent of the Fall Creek School District in Fall Creek, Wisconsin. The International Center for Leadership in Education named the Fall Creek School District a National Innovative District in 2016 and 2017. Joe started the #1minwalk2work Leadership Challenge, co-authored multiple books, including *Hacking Leadership: 10 Ways Great Leaders Inspire Learning That Teachers, Students, and Parents Love*, and most recently authored *Lead From Where You Are*. He was selected as one of fifty superintendents as a Personalized Learning Leader in 2016 by the U.S. Department of Education, and Education Dive named Joe their National Superintendent of the Year in 2019.

PREFACE
FROM FLAWED THINKING
TO NEW MINDSHIFTS

The way we see the problem is the problem.

—Stephen Covey (1989)

Embracing Mindshifts

Consciously choosing to think about old and ongoing problems in new and intentional ways is what we call a *mindshift*. This book is about mindshifts that educational leaders can make to generate new and necessary changes to established practices that currently aren't solving the important, urgent, and persistent issues within our schools—problems that should be approached with the same level of commitment and urgency as a crisis. In fact, we argue that there are perennial problems in education that have gone unresolved for so long that they have reached a crisis level. Our ultimate hope is that by demonstrating the flaws in the present thinking and by describing new ways of approaching old problems in education, you'll shift your mindset about how we do school.

> **Mindshift:** Consciously choosing to think about old and ongoing problems in new and intentional ways
> **Mindset:** A current mentality that influences how a leader perceives, thinks about, and reacts to a situation

We use the term *mindset* to reference a current mentality that influences how a leader perceives, thinks about, and reacts to a situation. Even when leaders have a "growth mindset," as defined by Dweck (2007), their perception and actions regarding old problems can still be limited by flawed thinking. Therefore, each chapter spotlights a new shift in thinking to a mindshift that is often used when faced with a crisis.

Each of the seven chapters follows a consistent structure that contains five distinct sections to help you analyze one mindshift at a time. Reflection questions are offered to close each chapter to help you process and connect the mindshift to your leadership role. The following describe each of the five sections per chapter and their purposes for readers.

 ## Outside Story

Inspiring leaders are found both within schools and within the corporate world. Every chapter of this book begins with a story that comes from outside of education that highlights how successful individuals and companies have exhibited the mindshift that the chapter will describe. These stories are not only meant to characterize the necessary thinking to initiate change but also provide the inspiration that change leadership and innovation are possible. New ways of leading are within our reach, and we have to look beyond the walls of our schools to find new ways of approaching old problems.

 ## Flawed Thinking

In each chapter, we provide you with a clear understanding as to why the current thought processes are unsuccessful in solving old problems. We take great lengths to explain how the prevailing logic, even the notions of making change, are failing to resolve our biggest and oldest problems. We have to come to terms with the fact that our best efforts aren't yielding the results that our most historically marginalized students need from their schools. You'll likely cringe as we candidly describe today's reality, even in systems that embrace the need to do things differently. As the chapters unfold, you will uncover why we believe that a mindshift is so desperately needed to combat our educational crises.

 New Mindshifts

This is the section where each chapter's mindshift is fully explored. We lay out a way of thinking about problems that will offer a fresh perspective and novel approaches to finding solutions. What we don't offer in this book are silver bullets or easy fixes to address your school's persistent problems; you need to know that before reading another word. We don't know your unique needs, and we don't propose to have all the answers. What we do offer are 7 mindshifts with a corresponding model for processing and solving lingering problems that will help you to move faster and more successfully toward your own solutions. We believe that this book, and what you can glean from it as a reader, is one of a kind. The models, as far as we know, have never been intentionally initiated in education before and only exist in other fields and in rare instances where success can be found.

Mindshifts and Their Models	
Mindshift	Model
Leading With a Crisis Mindset	Important, Urgent, and Persistent
Leading With a Battleground Mentality	Relentless, Experimental, Agile, and Learning Culture

(Continued)

Mindshifts and Their Models	
Mindshift	**Model**
Leading With a Beginner's Mind	Discover, Collect, Process, and Respond
Leading With an Octopus Approach	Learning, Independent Parts, Sensemaking, and Temperament (L.I.S.T.)
Leading With a Disciplined Tunnel Vision	Vision, Values, KPIs, Principles, Focus, and Models
Leading With a "Yes, And" Attitude	Define, Analyze, Identify, Select, Develop, Implement, and Evaluate
Leading With a "Go With What Is Known" Response	Accomplish, Understand, Decide, Initiate, and Test (A.U.D.I.T.)

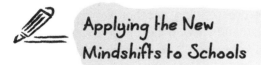

Applying the New Mindshifts to Schools

The mindshifts will apply to various problems that you might be facing. In this section of each chapter, we chose an obvious and persistent problem to which many school leaders will relate. While the provided connection aligns to only one problem, we expect that you will make your own connections to other problems that you face in your school or district. The mindshifts and their models are built to be used universally, but we apply them in each chapter as examples for how you might approach a needed change in your setting.

 ## Technical Tips

The technical tip at the end of each chapter is meant to help you get started in applying the mindshift to your school leadership role. We offer protocols, strategies, and techniques. Each will enable you to lead others in committing to eradicate persistent problems, preventing them from haunting our students, staff, and community yet another year in schools.

When you're done reading this book, you'll be a different kind of school leader than you are today. You'll learn to lead with a crisis mindset, and you'll attack old problems in new ways. You'll be less afraid, more empowered, and better equipped to challenge the status quo and do what needs to be done for our students. You will have reframed the concept of crisis in schools to see that persistent problems can only be solved if we approach them as the crises that they are.

Reframing "Crisis"

When you hear the word "crisis" you probably think of emergencies, catastrophes, or even a pandemic. And, rightly so. In addition to these single, but serious events, there are lingering and consequential problems in education that live in our schools, and we classify them as another type of crisis. As educators, authors, and consultants, we have the privilege of traveling the United States and working with schools in our own states and around the country; we see the same perennial problems afflicting schools year in and year out in school systems of every size and zip code. Educators have been fighting the same battles for decades, using the same thinking and the same tools with mixed results. Our central argument is that these issues have evolved into crisis proportions, and something new and different needs to be done about them.

Unfortunately, we also see some of our most deeply ingrained and inherent issues being left alone. And it's not because of ill-intended or apathetic leaders. What has happened over time is that our biggest issues have persisted for so long that we have grown accustomed to them. Maybe we even see them as a reality of our circumstances that is out of our control, conditions to accept or simply left as unsolvable given our current means. Whether it's a lack of resources or what seems to be an insurmountable effort, we find that busy school leaders have developed strategies and processes to *deal with* the outcomes of our most significant problems, but are just not able to *extinguish* them altogether. This, too, is becoming a crisis.

We can relate to how the day-to-day operations of a school or district can be so daunting that our mission to quell persistent problems takes a back seat to the problem du jour. This constant sense of urgency can create confusion on the difference between something that is an actual crisis and something that is important at the given moment. How we define a crisis is laid out in the first mindshift and threaded throughout the remaining chapters. In Chapter 1, you will find our three-part model that, when applied, will determine if an issue is in fact a crisis and should be dealt with accordingly using a new and intentional way of thinking about problems. We want leaders to know how and when to use what we call Leading with Crisis Mindset to make the difference that you intended to make when you became an educator. All of the other mindshifts in Chapters 2-7 are ways that we can lead with a crisis mindset to reach beyond the barriers of our oldest problems in schools. These are the mindshifts necessary to attack crises.

Feel the Shift

This book is written for school leaders—teachers, principals, and support staff—who care about leadership and the mindset that is needed to make a change. This book is for leaders who want to challenge the status quo in new ways. After reading this book, you will feel the following shifts:

1. *Think differently about old problems.* You'll understand why problems persist, and you'll shift to a new way of thinking about how to solve them.

2. *Discover new models for change.* We know that you are an instructional leader who supports a student-centered approach to equity for all kids. That's a given. What will help you, are the tools and tips for identifying the silent crises that are harming our schools and our students and the intentional mindset to eradicate them.

3. *Be equipped for change leadership.* We're inspired by literature regarding change leadership in education, and we know that this book will help leaders to initiate change by providing new ways of confronting our crises.

Leading With a Crisis Mindset

This book is a call to action for a new mindset for solving perennial problems in education, one where leaders follow a problem to its core and unveil every related issue and then work to build a comprehensive response that employs resources within the school and within the community. This new mindset for solving problems entirely and turning to systemic solutions is what we call a crisis mindset. We define it as *an unfiltered, 360° view, and approach to solving problems with urgency that abandons conventional wisdom and accepted restraints until a meaningful solution is found, implemented, and sustained.* It is an outlook and no-turning-back approach that responds with immediacy and urgency to old and ailing issues that are the Achilles heel of learning and progress in schools.

Leading with a Crisis Mindset is about finding new ways to think about old problems. With it comes new opportunities for engaging with our communities, accessing diverse resources, embracing radical new ideas, and charting a course of improvement—all actions designed to solve what is commonly held as an unsolvable issue. We challenge readers to consider long-standing problems in education as crises and approach them with the same tenacity that we did when the pandemic hit.

ACKNOWLEDGMENTS

Producing anything of value and substance requires a great deal of time and sacrifice. And, that time and sacrifice doesn't only come from those who are completing the work. In the case of this book, it came from the people closest to us—our families, friends, and colleagues, who are constant sources of encouragement, support, and inspiration. Without them, it simply wouldn't be possible to write or contribute beyond our daily work. With three people coauthoring this book, there are too many people who deserve acknowledgment to name. With that, we simply express our sincere gratitude to our family members, close friends, and coworkers for providing the support system needed to write this book.

We also want to thank and dedicate this book to all of the tremendous front-line educators and personnel who worked tirelessly throughout the pandemic to attend to student learning and well-being. Those in the trenches know how challenging the pandemic days were and the amount of effort and will that was required to maintain our connection with students. This book was inspired by the gravity of COVID-19 and how people responded to the huge demand for change that it required. Whether we look to teachers who made great strides in the classroom or to someone from nutritional services managing curbside food pickup, great efforts were made to reinvent what we once knew as the norm. Their commitment to students ignited in us an awareness and desire to identify what is possible when we make complete mindshifts about what we often accept as our reality.

At Corwin, thank you to Desirée Bartlett for letting us express our vision while pushing us to explore meaningful ways to connect with our readers.

Publisher's Acknowledgments

Corwin gratefully acknowledges the contributions of the following reviewers:

Ken Darvall, Principal
Tema International School (Ghana)
QLD, Australia

Joann Hulquist, Adjunct Professor, George Fox University
West Linn, OR

Louis Lim, Vice Principal
Ontario, Canada

Jacie Maslyk, Assistant Superintendent
Hopewell Area SD
Coraopolis, PA

Angela M. Mosley, Adjunct Professor
John Tyler Community College
Chester, VA

Lena Marie Rockwood, Assistant Principal
Revere High School
Los Angeles, CA

Joy Rose, Educational Consultant, Ohio ASCD Board of Directors
Worthington, OH

Franciene Sabens, School Counselor
Elkville, IL

Catherine Sosnowski
Torrington High School
Torrington, CT

Natalie R. Szakacs, Executive Senior Specialist, NIET
Rincon, GA

ABOUT THE AUTHORS

Connie Hamilton, EdS, served in the field of education for 25+ years as a teacher, instructional coach, principal, and central office administrator. She earned her master's and educational specialist degrees in the area of School Leadership with emphasis on curriculum and instruction. Her best-selling book *Hacking Questions: 11 Answers That Create a Culture of Inquiry in Your Classroom* was published in 2019. Along with Starr Sackstein, she coauthored *Hacking Homework: 10 Strategies that Inspire Learning Outside the Classroom* and also wrote *Strained and Drained: Tools for Overworked Teachers* with coauthor, Dorothy VanderJagt. Throughout her career, Connie has supported teachers and administrators to refine their instructional practices and be reflective educators. With experience throughout K-12, Connie is mindful of systemic needs and how to develop structures that create growth within the entire system. Connie presents internationally on topics centered around instructional practices such as questioning, formative assessment, teacher clarity, and student engagement. Leaders and teachers benefit from Connie's experience when she coaches them to put practice to action as they continue to learn and grow.

Joseph Jones, EdD, is the Superintendent of the New Castle County Vocational-Technical School District in Delaware. Joe is a former high school social studies teacher, assistant principal, and principal. As principal, he was named the Delaware Secondary Principal of the Year and during his tenure, Delcastle Technical High School was the first high school to receive the state's Outstanding Academic Achievement Award. He received his doctorate from the University of Delaware in Educational Leadership and was awarded the Outstanding Doctoral Student Award of his class. He presents nationally on topics of school leadership and is the cofounder of the leadership development institute, TheSchoolHouse302. Along with T.J. Vari, he coauthored *Candid and Compassionate Feedback: Transforming Everyday Practice in Schools*. And, with Salome Thomas-EL and T.J. Vari, he coauthored *Passionate Leadership: Creating a Culture of Success in Every School, Building a Winning Team: The Power of a Magnetic Reputation and the Need to Recruit Top Talent in Every School*, and *Retention for a Change: Motivate, Inspire, and Energize Your School Culture*.

T.J. Vari, EdD, is the Assistant Superintendent of Secondary Schools and District Operations in the Appoquinimink School District in Delaware. He is a former middle school assistant principal and principal and former high school English teacher and department chair. His master's degree is in School Leadership and his doctorate is in Innovation and Leadership where he accepted the Award for Academic Excellence given to one doctoral student per graduating class. He holds several honors and distinctions, including his past appointment as President of the Delaware Association for School Administrators, his work with the Delaware Association for School Principals, and the honor in accepting the Paul Carlson Administrator of the Year Award. His efforts span beyond the K-12 arena into higher education where he holds adjunct appointments, teaching courses at the master's and doctoral level. He is a national presenter on topics of school leadership and a Cofounder of TheSchoolHouse302, a leadership development institute. Along with Joseph Jones, he coauthored *Candid and Compassionate Feedback: Transforming Everyday Practice in Schools*. And, with Salome Thomas-EL and Joseph Jones, he coauthored *Passionate Leadership: Creating a Culture of Success in Every School*, *Building a Winning Team: The Power of a Magnetic Reputation and the Need to Recruit Top Talent in Every School*, and *Retention for a Change: Motivate, Inspire, and Energize Your School Culture*.

INTRODUCTION
FINDING NEW WAYS TO THINK ABOUT OLD PROBLEMS

By focusing my attention on the solution to the problem rather than the problem, I was able to quickly turn what seemed like a major crisis into an opportunity.

—Les Brown (2007)

Ghosts of Underperformance

Although there are varying theories regarding the purpose of schools as institutions within American culture, evidenced by the myriad of school vision and mission statements that exist today, most agree that schools are designed for three key reasons. First, schools are expected to create a knowledgeable and skilled workforce that can productively contribute to our dynamic society. This means that schools have a universal economic function to provide people with the skills and abilities to be employable and to contribute to the goods and services needed to sustain our communities. Second, schools are supposed to focus on the global implications of the society in which we live, including each individual's growth, both academically and morally, so that we can comprehend and achieve new ways of living that are both comfortable and sustainable. Third, schools exist to help people as they grow and mature to realize their full potential. Education and learning, when done well, should honor individuals and support them to grow into the best version of their true selves.

1

Each sentiment is forged in the notion that school is designed for the preparation one needs to live making their own contributions to the greater world outside of education. While one aspect of the equation is about jobs, another is focused on humanity itself, and the last, maybe most important, is about self-awareness and being fulfilled. Nonetheless, these beliefs about schooling demonstrate a desire for schools to develop and strengthen every student's capacity as a human. There are all kinds of other arguments to be made about the purpose of school, *and* the underlying concept is that school should prepare young people for their futures, and many of the current metrics used for school accountability have identified that schools are not succeeding as they were intended.

In fact, for almost three quarters of a century, the American education system has been criticized as underperforming. In 1958 *Life* magazine contrasted a student from Chicago to his Soviet counterpart. This led to a major reform of schools in the United States. However, schools left serious problems untouched and the status of schools in the United States compared to other countries declined. Arne Duncan, a former Secretary of Education and veteran of the Chicago public school system, started the first sentence in his 2019 book, *How Schools Work: An Inside Account of Failure and Success from One of the Nation's Longest-Serving Secretaries of Education* with, "Education runs on lies." The widespread belief that the American education system is not working is not a new phenomenon.

We don't believe that this general attitude is a condemnation of educators but rather a hard look at the system itself. Certainly, there remains faith that schools can and will improve despite the growing number who believe the public school system is beyond repair. Too many schools are haunted year-in and year-out with the same obstacles and challenges that they seemingly can't overcome or, quite frankly, that they have accepted as reality. Determined leaders use their best skills to turn schools around, one complex problem at a time. From literacy scores to student discipline, from teacher retention to dropout rates, from poverty to lack of funding, there are countless issues that schools in the United States contend with every day.

Schools are a microcosm that uniquely display all of society's problems and yet their leaders are put in a position to solve them when no other federal, state, or local agency has been able to do so. Just let that validation soak in for a moment. It's about the most unfair expectation that has been heaped upon any single public enterprise, and as school leaders we are at the head of it. As lifelong educators, committed to students and staff, this is the challenging reality that shakes us to our core. The ghosts of underperformance continue to haunt our educational institution today and will do so for the foreseeable future. That is, unless we think about these issues with a mindset that has never been used before.

Perennial Problems in Education

Consider common perpetual issues within education—crises such as numeracy, equity, grading, reading ability, and teacher retention—that are continually managed but not solved for future sustainability. A prime example is student apathy. Once this attitude evolves into disruptive behavior, tardiness, and absenteeism, it can have disastrous consequences as a gateway for student dropout. Many schools are managing this well, on a daily basis, but we're a long way from a long-term resolution across every system.

The challenge that we face is that many of our interventions and meaningful approaches are one-sided, with most of the work being done by the school staff alone. Unfortunately, because these problems are so complex in nature, and, in the case of apathy—the student possibly unwilling, unable, or even unavailable to be included in the solution—the responsibility defaults to the school and not necessarily anyone or anything else that should be factored into a meaningful change.

This means that more phone calls, more meetings, and, frankly, more consequences rarely work, impacting more greatly a marginalized population of students as it stands. This is the type of problem that needs to be approached and solved through a different mindset, what we call a *crisis mindset*. Our central argument in this book is that the perennial problems that persist in education will never truly change unless we approach them as we would an in-the-moment crisis. If there was a fire in the dumpster behind the school, we wouldn't schedule a meeting about it or form a committee. We would be all hands on deck, including the local first responders, to put the fire out. Then, we would investigate the reason for the fire to put systems in place so that it won't happen again. That's not how we currently treat student apathy, reading scores, absenteeism, and other chronic issues. But it should be.

Chronic Conditions for Failure

Many of the attempts to solve these deeply ingrained problems aren't actual solutions at all but rather efforts for coping with the problems in the best way we know how. The multitude of strategies that have been used to improve third-grade reading scores, for example, are as effective as a fork in a sugar bowl. Mindshifts are necessary, ones that seek to identify and treat every aspect of a problem. Our sugar bowl needs a shovel.

Most attempts at solving major problems in education are limited by two chronic conditions for failure: One, they are transactional by design; and two, they fail to recruit and extend solutions beyond the walls of the school. Let's take a closer look at our literacy example. We know that it's a key determiner of student success in school and life (Ritchie & Bates, 2013). Yet, many students continue to read below grade level even when literacy is the focus of every teacher and support staff. Why haven't our school improvement plans been effective?

THE TRANSACTION

To improve lifelong literacy, many schools will purchase a viable program and recruit a dynamic teacher to lead the charge. This approach is transactional. The identified problem is a lack of rigorous reading, and the treatment is a new reading program. Let's assume that this process works—done well and implemented coherently (Fullan & Quinn, 2016)—the reading program has the potential to improve reading scores for students who lack proficiency within that single school. The chronic condition is not a lack of effort from the school, but, rather, the scalability of the solution and its sustainability within the system.

In this case, the improved reading scores are a confined victory, dependent upon leadership, resources, and talent that are unique to the school. The response is reactionary and only addresses the problem in one specific school. This type of solution does nothing to address the causes for inadequate reading scores, and therefore, only acts on *effects* of a systemic issue but doesn't combat the *root causes* to prevent it from recurring within future populations of students. Figure I.1 shows how the root causes are unseen and do not have easy access. The effects, in this image the leaves, are more visible and can be reached with less effort. Using this analogy, it's understandable that when schools are awarded grants to tend to the leaves of the problem—analyze data, buy new programs, develop staff skills—they find that when the grant money runs out, the problem remains or recurs. The deeply rooted problems in education require permanent solutions to completely abolish the undesired outcomes.

This typical response to a symptom, in Figure I.1 the leaves, such as expecting a reading program to solve low achievement, accommodates the real problem within that school. But it neglects to address literacy issues systematically. Chances are, the problem does not originate within the school— therefore, it cannot be solved there. One might contend that third-grade reading scores are primarily a result of reading deficiencies that stem from the time when the child was

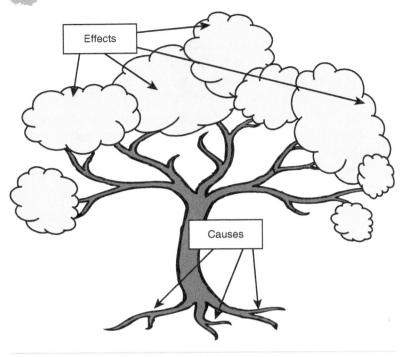

Image source: Clker-free-vectorimages/pixabay.com

younger than five. In that case, the foundational issue is not the scores, but rather circumstances outside the realm of K-12. Only by diagnosing the true problem can leaders then take actions for abolishing the problem. However, if the root cause is found to be lack of exposure to complex texts once students learn the fundamentals of reading, strategies to increase time that children are engaged with challenging texts can be explored.

Einstein is reported to have said that if he only had one hour to solve a problem he would spend 55 minutes defining the problem and five minutes on the solution. With this in mind, jumping to a conclusion that teachers need training on a new literacy program will not address the root cause of lack of exposure to texts be it prekindergarten or during school. It's a mismatch. The strategy does not align with the problem. It's effectively the same as changing your oil because you have a flat tire. This awareness of problem-solution alignment is precisely the type of clarity we offer.

Educators are better positioned to create systemic solutions when underlying issues are laid bare. We'll say more about this in Chapter 5. Nonetheless, we don't want to minimize school-based successes; school leaders should attack their individual problems as best they can. There is no doubt that real wins occur under herculean efforts, but wouldn't systemic responses be preferable so that the herculean efforts aren't necessary? Reactionary thinking is exhausting and will never stem the tide of a problem that has its origin elsewhere. Instead, we advocate for mindshifts that aim to uproot problems at their origin once and for all.

THE NEED FOR A NETWORK

This leads us to the crux of the second chronic condition for failure, which is trying to solve the problem solely within the walls of the school. The problems that are haunting schools year-in and year-out are also plaguing communities across the country. Anywhere we find poverty, we also find internet connectivity issues. Schools can't solve these problems alone. A network of support composed of the school and outside supporting agencies is needed for lasting and sustainable change. With a shared responsibility between the community and the school, each party bears the role of problem-solver and can embrace problems rather than pawn them off. Pairing resources accomplishes things that could never be achieved alone.

There are situations when the school and community agencies are restricted because they are governmentally controlled. Yes, policies, legislation, and funding are critical, but it is also important to note that solutions do not live solely within the walls of the legislative hall. Community organizations, from businesses to after-school programs, need to work in unison, and mutually accept these challenges as everyone's responsibility with joint accountability for the solutions. This does not take the burden from the school and place it elsewhere. In fact, the school leader might act as the primary influencer. It just signifies a change in mindset that the chronic conditions for failure are perpetuated by the one-to-one transactions that individual schools believe will allow them to solve problems that, in actuality, are far beyond what school reform could possibly accomplish. Perennial issues in education, our Ghosts of Underperformance, won't be solved if both of the chronic conditions for failure aren't reworked. We advocate for a new way of thinking.

A Network of Support

If we genuinely want to help schools succeed, then communities as a whole must abandon the typical finger-pointing approach to problem-solving and embrace the truth that innovation and genius are discovered when we are willing to be vulnerable, when we admit to our shortcomings, and when we partner with others to solve our problems (Brown, 2015). We currently only see this phenomenon—vulnerability, acceptance, and partnership—when a community is facing a crisis.

The care that many people receive from community members when diagnosed with an illness is an example that comes to mind. An individual receives expert attention from doctors and may even require extended care in a hospital. But the hospital team doesn't come over and cut the patient's grass or feed the patient's dog—friends and neighbors do that work. If the person doesn't have someone to watch the children, family members take over, not the hospital. It's not the nurse who drops off the pan of lasagna; it's a concerned coworker. The ideal community provides a complete network of support, and the network doesn't come together just to help with the illness. Everyone realizes that there are peripheral needs in addition to medical treatment, and each person or entity plays their necessary role.

When friends and family aren't available, we've also witnessed what happens. Things fall apart. All those needs don't go away, and they become severe issues that, when unresolved over time, become very complicated to reverse. The doctors and hospitals aren't able to solve all of these problems for their patients. They may have contacts and resources for the patient, but their primary purpose is to treat the patient's illness.

In contrast, think about what happens in schools. As community resources become scarce, schools have evolved into doing far more than just educating students, offering services that are generally well beyond the scope of the school's purpose. This is specifically where the community network is needed. Schools aren't balking or rejecting these new and growing demands, but they do require that the neighbor come over to cut the grass or that someone help out after hours to make sure everything is in working order. This is mostly so that the schools can focus on the job of educating children. This give-and-take relationship also works in reverse when schools serve as supporters for the community. School facilities can be used for community education and youth athletics or hosting a food drive for the local food pantry. The point is, during times of crisis, we develop networks of support—that's exactly what is needed in schools. We need to see these perennial problems as the crises they are and apply the mindshifts to address them.

Opportunity From Crisis

The word "crisis" immediately elicits an emotional response. However, if we trace the word "crisis" back to its Latin and Greek roots, we find that it refers to a turning point. The turning point occurs because of the response to a crisis, which is where we find an intensified level of human thinking and action. The collaboration, commitment, strength, innovation, and focus are unparalleled. We are not referring to the primal reactions that many people have during a crisis that cloud judgment, cause panic, and limit resourceful thinking. We are delving into the minds of the people who somehow find clarity and rise to provide needed leadership in a crisis. This type of crisis-thinking is attributed to leaders of our past, like Abraham Lincoln and Martin Luther King, Jr. but also business leaders of the present, like Patrick Doyle, who we feature later in Chapter 7.

To understand this type of thinking better, we must first determine what constitutes a crisis. As humans, we respond to situations and events in a variety of ways. Typically, we hope that our reaction is equal to the severity of the circumstances at hand. Not everything is a crisis, and we're not saying that leaders should use a crisis mindset at all times, quite the contrary. Some problems are small and easily managed, while others have the potential to be completely disruptive. Some issues affect a small number of people while others can alter entire communities and countries forever. The size of the problem, the magnitude of the disruption, and how many people are impacted are not what make for a crisis.

Even the severity of the problem alone doesn't qualify it to be a crisis. The problem itself is only one side of the equation, and the other side is whether or not there are resources in place or enough people who are capable and available to deal with the circumstances. It's at this intersection—available resources and human capacity to handle the problem—where we find ourselves in crisis. In other words, a crisis is an event that, left to its natural progression, is unmanageable. Without a new way of thinking and a new level of support, a crisis will continue to devastate everyone in its path.

Lessons Learned From the Pandemic

One thing that we've learned from various crises in history, and most recently COVID-19 in 2020, is that humans will move mountains to find short-term solutions that can have implications for long-term sustainability. When events threaten to crumble the foundation on which we live, we respond to preserve and protect our well-being and ultimately our survival. During COVID-19, we have seen incredible reactions and changes made in record time to respond to life-threatening scenarios. We've seen alliances made, locally and nationally, for the betterment of humanity. We've witnessed amazing creativity and accelerated innovation.

These changes speak to healthcare facilities, small business, restaurant owners, and more. Particularly within education, we've seen transformation in processes and teaching strategies that literally shifted within days and sometimes hours. It's true that some of these changes were on the horizon anyway, while changes might not have happened for decades. The pandemic taught us that we have the capacity to tackle our most intractable issues. But this was only possible with the kind of determination and mental shift that we don't usually manifest on a daily basis.

MINDSHIFT #1: LEADING WITH A CRISIS MINDSET

Close scrutiny will show that most of these everyday so-called "crisis situations" are not life or death matters at all, but opportunities to advance, or stay where you are.

—Maxwell Maltz (1976)

Outside Story: Unconventional Decisions

On the surface it seems like Zappos is just another shoe and clothing distribution company. That's what they do, but it's not who they are. If you take a moment to learn about the company, you'll realize that they are completely consumer-focused. A real Zappos super-fan knows that they're essentially a warehouse company committed to being an elite customer service provider—handling inventory and customer satisfaction at a superior level.

Zappos' success didn't come easily. There was a time when the company outsourced their warehouse and storage facilities. This made it difficult to accurately assess their inventory or delivery time—two nightmares for a company dependent on speed of delivery and consumer relationships. While other businesses might have focused on trying to perfect outsourcing to save money, Zappos moved to owning and operating their own warehouses. While other companies may have sunk more money into services that customers enjoyed, Zappos shifted their entire operation to support its call center and the staffing needs for phone reps.

We selected Zappos' to spark your thinking because they did three things that most organizations fail to do. One, they didn't see their current strategy as the only path to success, refusing to continue dumping money and resources into a failing strategy. They pivoted, fast and hard. Two, they understood the implications of change, both the positive and the potentially negative. It's not easy to pick a new place for your company to call home, yet, that's what they did a couple times. Once they moved to Kentucky next to the UPS World-Port to open a fulfillment center, and then they moved to Henderson, Nevada, to solve their call center issues. Knowing that many employees might not be willing to make the trek with them, they made the tough decision to move to an area that would support the growth and vision of the company. Three, they confronted the crisis with new and different thinking to measure success. While other companies rely on metrics like how long a representative will be on the phone with someone, Zappos ignores traditional metrics and focuses on customer satisfaction through incredible customer service.

Zappos abandoned traditional thinking and conventional wisdom to lead with a crisis mindset with the following:

1. When something isn't working, pivot fast and hard.

2. Radical change is a tough decision, do it anyway.

3. Confront the crisis with new thinking, abandon traditional measures.

Flawed Thinking: The Lost Opportunities

There are two prevailing issues with how we work to solve problems in education. One, our solutions conform to our current school system, which imposes limitations. In fact, it can actually prevent our brains from seeing breakthroughs and opportunities. We call this *Dimmed Lights*. Two, our approach to solving problems usually is in the form of altering instruction, using programs, and increasing our professional prowess. Yet, we rarely take the necessary time to really learn the initiative, allow it to affect change, and implement it with fidelity. We call this the *Starting Block Syndrome*. Let's unpack the reasons for both.

THE DIMMED LIGHTS PHENOMENON

Our brains do a tremendous job, completely involuntary, on spotlighting and dimming certain areas of interest as well as filtering out other irrelevant data. This filtration process is phenomenal as the brain deletes, dismisses, and dims things that are immaterial so that it can illuminate those areas that are relevant and critical. Consider how important this function is in our daily lives. Routine skills, like driving a car, are made possible through our ability to focus on the road and the other cars as we drive on a highway all the while eliminating the unnecessary distractions that would otherwise capture our attention. We may notice a billboard or beautiful tree, but it passes by as we center on those more important specifics, such as a stoplight or a pedestrian.

Whether driving a car or teaching in a classroom, our senses— touch, smell, taste, hearing, and sight—are bombarded with an inordinate amount of information. We function on our brain's ability to perform its task of zooming in on some items and clouding out others. It's fascinating how much new information is being gathered about the brain as new technologies in the field of neuroscience are emerging. Recent advances have revealed that the brain functions differently than we originally believed. What was once thought to be true about how the brain focuses on particular features of our world is actually the opposite. Instead, the brain is remarkably good at dulling what is deemed as nonessential. What we now know is that "the brain wasn't brightening the light on stimuli of interest; it was lowering the lights on everything else" (Cepelewicz, 2019).

This is a profound discovery when we think about what to focus on to improve our schools and how. Since, we naturally dim the light on the areas that we don't perceive as vital, the conclusions we draw about school improvement, whether a literacy initiative or parental involvement, are dependent on our brain's natural ability to isolate and obscure other information. Looking at this through an educational leadership lens, we see how this phenomenon plays out. The lights are simply being lowered in certain areas within classrooms, schools, and districts, potentially making it difficult to see possibilities of unique change and unconventional decisions that lie beyond our central focus. This is not done intentionally, actually quite the opposite. Schools are built and designed to grow learners within a prescribed construct that is intended for a large body of students. The general process of schooling is to take preidentified information and skills that are aligned to a set of standards and transform them into practical classroom instruction. This is precisely how we miss opportunities.

At the earliest levels of education, students learn integral skills, such as reading, so that they can eventually use the skill of reading to learn. The system is built to equip students to learn key information, develop skills to use that information, and then expand those skills to extend their own thinking. The major challenge in this process is that the structures for learning and the educational system itself is complex, making change slow and arduous. The system doesn't naturally shift when we encounter struggling students, adverse challenges, and seemingly insurmountable situations that lie beyond the established norm and traditional construct. When students are struggling with concepts, ideas, and skills, or even with behaving and cooperating with others, we don't look at altering the system, but rather we work to infuse support and services within the predesigned system to assist the child.

As such, the process for learning doesn't change; rather, we simply add to it. This can come in the form of programs, extra time, extra help, specifically designed instruction, etc. You name it, schools have done it. All these additions help to support student improvement to some degree, but they are designed to help the student within the provided school construct, which, in and of itself, may be the limiting factor. We don't abandon the mold; we simply work within it. We rarely arrive at the essential question: what if the mold is wrong for the student? In the case where the answer is "yes," all of the structures and supports that we add will only have a minimal positive effect because they are designed within an inflexible predetermined framework.

This is not to suggest that educators aren't fully committed to student improvement or that we should abandon our way of schooling altogether. Rather, we must recognize how our system of schooling imposes limitations and contributes to how we view problems. Our perception may be obscured by how we naturally focus on some things and not others. It means that we need to quit thinking within the proverbial box or in this case the schoolhouse to solve ailing issues.

It also reveals that providing an education to every child is arguably more challenging than ever. Given the complexities of our society and the diverse needs of every community, the educational system has to become far more elastic in nature. Schools strive to not only provide rigorous instruction but also seamlessly create a responsive classroom designed to assess student needs for greater academic progress. But altering modes of instruction to best meet the needs of every student in real time within the current construct of the system is notably impossible. It's just that, impossible, and to be candid, doing what we've always done isn't going to get us to what can be possible.

The issues become most prominent when students' needs fall outside and beyond that of the traditional track designed within the system. Unfortunately, the constraints within the system may be the barrier to the students' development and growth. The educational system, something we refer to as the educational industrial complex in Chapter 2, can be so rigid that it prevents alternative paths for student learning, who don't follow the normal course of grade-level age-determined standards. To work around this reality, schools often use tools and programs that they believe can work within the system and also increase student achievement. However, this strategy is riddled with its own issues.

THE STARTING BLOCK SYNDROME

To understand this further, consider the sport of track and field. One of the most important tools for a track and field runner is the starting blocks. Exceptional sprinters use the blocks to their advantage and practice extensively on how to come out of the blocks appropriately. Great sprinters' per-formance is highly correlated with their start time (Bezodis, Willwacher, & Salo, 2019). However, the blocks alone are not what makes the sprinter faster, but it is the effective use of the blocks and the sprinter's reaction time as the gun sounds.

In 2021, the fastest man on the planet is Usain Bolt with a remarkable 100-meter time of 9.58 seconds (Nag, 2020). However, in the 2017 world championship in London, Bolt finished third. Although he covered the ground faster than anyone else on the track, his starting block time was milli-seconds slower than Justin Goleman and Christian Catlin (The Speed Project, 2021). The blocks can serve as a major advantage or disadvantage. There is no doubt that they help, but the proper use of them is critical whether you are an elite world-class sprinter or a competitive high school athlete. What is designed to help and offer support needs to also be mastered to become effective in its use. In fact, introducing a young or inexperienced runner to the blocks too soon could do more harm than good.

In similar fashion, schools implement tools and strategies that could prove to be highly effective, but without adequate time to learn and master them or modify the setting, we miss the opportunity to fully experience their power. We refer to this as the starting block syndrome because although these tools and strategies may yield results, they certainly won't do so if they're not used effectively. For example, teachers often find themselves with a new reading series, or a new math program, or even professional learning on high leverage instruction that they must fit into their day. Coupling this with our natural focus to work within our prescribed daily timeframe, we naturally dim or cancel out other problems. The tool or strategy becomes the primary focus and is viewed as the solution. Again, it's the proper use of the starting blocks—new tools and strategies—not the blocks alone. We've learned throughout COVID-19, and other crises, that with the proper mindset, we won't stop adjusting our approach, and we can continue to tweak the use of a strategy until we achieve our goals.

This common method of adding tools and strategies to fix issues fails to provide the necessary support to fully develop the teachers' knowledge and skills to meet the students' needs. It only results in another weak attempt to resolve a difficult problem, and we find ourselves on a treadmill of strategy-based adjustments in the use of tools and new tricks that end up falling short. If the training for these modifications remains at an introductory level, we can expect that teachers will lack the differentiated professional learning that is needed to cultivate expertise. This is not a teacher problem, but it's a system problem. If teachers get the blocks, but they can't push from them the way that's needed, the blocks are not helpful. The strategy ends up being absorbed into the classroom and used as a support mechanism. It becomes a treatment for the problem, not a real solution. Ultimately, the one-size-fits-all training and the program-based method of adding more to the already complicated and overworked system produces limited results with increased frustration.

The question then becomes how can we break free from this cycle of identifying a problem, providing limited treatment by adding to the already overflowing workload, and expecting improved results, only to see minor improvements if any? The answer begins with our ability to embrace a crisis mindset in schools. Each decision that we believe will improve outcomes that must be governed by key strategies and driven by a set of central activities. We can't continue to add programs or implement initiatives that lack the professional training needed for them to be successful or that simply heap more onto our educators as the single variable in a very complex formula.

And, the magnitude of the effort must mirror the size of the crisis itself. Hoping that the new curriculum will solve our equity and access issues is an empty promise at best. Lastly, to shift our approach and completely alter our mindset for solving perennial problems, we must first confront our own relationship with what we have for so long deemed as insurmountable challenges within the system.

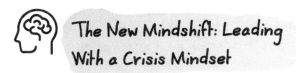

The New Mindshift: Leading With a Crisis Mindset

By continuing to use the same common approaches to our persistent problems, we fail to see the unique approaches necessary to make a difference. The problems are persistent and the tools and strategies that we're using to solve them haven't changed. Unfortunately, the very institutions that are charged with teaching students to use creativity aren't using a creative approach to its own issues. We've dulled the wrong sensory inputs. We hate to say it, but we've become comfortably numb.

Leading with a Crisis Mindset means responding with immediacy and urgency to old and ailing issues that would otherwise continue to be the Achilles heel of learning, progress, and new paths to success in schools.

To break free from the traditional approach of solving problems requires what we describe as a crisis mindset. A shift to a new mindset for solving problems and creating systemic solutions: *an unfiltered 360° view and approach to solving problems with urgency that abandons conventional wisdom and accepts restraints until a meaningful solution is found, implemented, and sustained.* It is an attitude about problems that includes a no-turning-back approach. Leading with a Crisis Mindset means responding with immediacy and urgency to old and ailing issues that would otherwise continue to be the Achilles' heel of learning, progress, and new paths to success in schools.

There are three primary reasons for why this has occurred in education, probably true for other failing industries as well. The first is that the system is immovable, stuck in its ways, and heavily bureaucratic. The paths to real and continued success aren't clear enough for all stakeholders to agree on and pursue. Granted, some schools and systems have developed an out-of-the-box means for experiencing success, but too often these means aren't scalable and dissolve with turnover. It's time to move past what we know, beyond traditional approaches, and onto new ways of thinking about these old problems. The second is that we don't spend enough time thinking about our relationship with internal problems. Why aren't we able to see past the problem itself? Without this type of metacognition, we're doomed to a loop of poor self-efficacy and fear that we can't solve problems or that change is unsafe and feels wrong. The lack of comfort can be disturbing if we're truly forging a new path. And third, we haven't confronted our crises as such and that means that we won't initiate the urgency and resolve needed for change. As

Fullan stated (1993), "the insurmountable problem is juxta-posing a continuous change theme with a continuous conser-vative system that defies change. In partnership with all community agencies, educators must initiate the creation of learning societies as part of a larger social agenda."

This agenda not only needs to be fully inclusive of several key stakeholders, but it must also face perennial problems with a brave new approach, a crisis mindset, to forever move the needle of performance in schools.

PROBLEM-SOLVING, CREATIVITY, AND NEW PATHS TO SUCCESS

The ingenuity in our ability to solve problems stems from our willingness and devotion to uncovering new paths to success. But it's not natural for our brains to search for new and uncomfortable routines. In fact, when we are forced to solve issues that lie outside of our typical setting, we must rely on a unique and innovative resolve that not everyone has or that we don't commonly employ. As Gopnik (2011) puts it, "as we get older our brains 'prune out' the weaker, less used path-ways and strengthen the ones that are used most often." This is particularly challenging when we need to rely on "imagi-nation" and "creativity" to solve complex issues that require "out of the box" divergent thinking. Because the problems require new and creative thinking is, in part, a problem itself. Routines and established processes won't change without a mindshift.

In March of 2020, schools faced an unprecedented and unpredictable predicament. With almost no warning, the institutions where learning takes place—including colleges and universities, preschool programs, and K-12 systems—were considered fertile environments for the spread of a deadly virus. Schools closed for what was meant to be a short two-week break but what turned into a situation without any clarity or end in sight. School systems were forced to find ways to educate children beyond the school. The challenges were endless, and the solutions weren't readily available. Kitchen tables became virtual learning spaces. Teachers' technological skills were accelerated by necessity. Schools didn't just need 1:1 devices for students, but also they needed to ensure at-home connectivity.

Educators were forced to embrace a different approach to problem-solving. Teachers surprised themselves by doing whatever it took to reach and teach children effectively in a very unfamiliar (understatement) environment. There was a benefit to this shift in thinking because it resulted in a shift in strategies for finding solutions to problems that had been ineffectively tackled for years.

Educators and other professions, who were suddenly thrust into a new and different reality than ever before, were obligated to change in order to continue. Some quit shortly after coming to a realization that they weren't equipped for the changes that needed to be made. Others learned to cope with the speed at which they needed to learn new ways of engaging students. Some, because of years of investing in themselves with new technologies and updated practices, were able to seamlessly integrate all of the newness, even helping others as they could.

OUR RELATIONSHIP WITH CRISES

To understand a crisis mindset conceptually, we must first analyze our relationship and innate human tendencies when it comes to crises. First, our responses to challenging issues often commensurate with our belief in ourselves and the systems in which we work. This is similar to how Dweck (2015) describes our responses to certain situations in terms of the limitations we place on our abilities due to a *fixed mindset*. Whether we realize it or not, our ability to successfully face and solve a problem is limited and thwarted before we ever begin to solve it. Our mindset is the prohibitive factor in being creative about new solutions because it guides our approach.

Second, people like to feel safe. Psychological safety is the topic of a number of new studies regarding how people can become more vulnerable at work to be able to contribute more in an environment that accepts failure (Brown, 2015). But, there's a problem when psychological safety is a delusion. In the case of perennial problems, feeling safe to continue doing as we've always done without applying new ideas and solutions is fake. It's a false impression. Our action creates safety when it shouldn't. This is how our relationship with crises fails us from the start. Because we are so desperate for a feeling of safety, we create it even when it doesn't exist.

In this regard, our relationship with crises—our self-efficacy about solving problems and our frantic need for safety—forestalls progress. If we truly believe an issue cannot be solved, perhaps only managed, then we will never find a resolution. Our focus is misplaced. Our brain's natural course of action will not be solution-driven but rather control-driven. This is why understanding how we perceive and respond to a crisis is imperative. The common approaches and efforts, despite their lack of success, will continue. There's more safety in continuing what doesn't work than admitting that we've had it all wrong, that something, more than likely drastic, needs to change. Efforts will push forward, and the status quo will remain. A concessional belief that "it's better than not doing anything" will prevail.

For educators to evaluate whether or not we can handle and solve certain problems is the first step in determining our path forward. This has been confused in the past—mostly by politicians and theorists—as a lack of will or a lack of skill, which we have found to be incorrect. This is why under-standing our relationship with crises is imperative. We have to metacognitively gauge whether or not the reasons we accept the status quo are due to the limits of our self- and collective efficacy, whether it's our need for safety, and if we can push past both toward something new. In coming to terms with our relationship with crises, we can see crises for what they are, not some insurmountable problems, rather prob-lems that we need more help solving. We're reminded of the chronic conditions for failure in that it's okay to admit that we can't solve a problem in education as long as we're willing to recruit other institutions for help.

In *Becoming Bulletproof* (2020), Eva Poumpouras tells readers how fear can limit our ability to live a full life, prevent us from pursuing our goals, and, at its worst, rob us from the joy of day-to-day living. This is the essence of our relationship with crises and the reason why education is numbed by the fear of admitting that we aren't doing what is best for every student. We aren't. What comes next is the important part—the mindshift to leading with a crisis mindset.

CONFRONTING A CRISIS

Consider how often we establish a goal to increase English Language Arts (ELA) and Math student achievement scores. We institute clear and identifiable metrics, how much the aggregate and disaggregate need to improve, and we even have a clear knowledge of the gap in performance among subgroups. Even with all of this clarity and meaningful data, this approach will more likely yield little success. Embracing the crisis and its magnitude is the first step to confronting it and solving the problem, not goal-setting and strategic planning. Identifying the needs of the students within the context of learning is the key to improving outcomes; setting goals based on a test score is not the same as educating every child.

Regardless as to whether we're talking about No Child Left Behind or Every Student Succeeds Act, effective school leaders quickly realize that the test scores neglect to tell the real story about many of the fundamental needs of our students. Most students who need test score improvements have other more demanding requirements before we can apply an after-school tutoring program, for example. This is why confronting the crisis first, before setting the test score goals, is so critical. Even answering the question: "what's the crisis?" with "test scores" is only half true. If we don't know what the problem is, we can't fix it.

As Garvin (1993) stated, "In the absence of learning, companies—and individuals—simply repeat old practices. Change remains cosmetic, and improvements are either fortuitous or short-lived." In the case of education, change efforts are primarily about what and how to teach. In recent years, we've made strides toward a clearer picture about neuroscience and how the brain functions to learn, but we're still unlocking the use of social and emotional learning strategies to truly get at the heart of who students are and how we can help them to carve their own educational journey. It's their sense of self at school that might matter more than the schooling they receive.

This is what we mean by confronting the crisis, unraveling the problem before naming solutions and setting goals. The whole idea is to immerse ourselves in the information we have and then begin to develop answers to new questions without any of the traditional limiting constraints. Let's use graduation requirements as one of those constraints. Because students need four years of ELA, we will often enroll students in ninth-grade English, all at some level, to ensure that they obtain the credit. However, what if the ninth-grade student reads at a seventh-grade level? Our response is to provide additional help—after-school programs, perhaps a reading specialist to work with the teacher, maybe a more sophisticated program to help differentiate reading levels. All are noble. Some may come with a degree of success. But, the issue remains that they don't directly attack the problem. The crisis persists and the next student comes along, reading at a sixth-grade level. The system is a mouse on a wheel, unable to slow down for long enough to step off and truly evaluate if the wheel is even going anywhere. Instead, we stick to what we know, we crave safety in what we do, and we cloud our vision from the crises that are in our presence each day.

In reading this book, we hope to change your mind, shift your thinking, and help you to see the crises we have in education, perennial problems that aren't going anywhere unless we learn to lead with a new mindset. We know that we can help you with a different framework for approaching problems; we also know that we can't solve them for you. This isn't a solution book, and you need to know that moving forward. It's a problem-solving guide for your most difficult issues in education. The only people who can solve a school's problems are the people who work there and the community in which the school resides. With all of the professional development that we, as consultants, provide for schools and districts each year, we know one thing: it's what they do when we leave that matters most. So, you're probably asking yourself this important question: How do we distinguish problems as crises from other emergent issues that leaders need to address? We have a model for that.

MODEL: IMPORTANT, URGENT, AND PERSISTENT

Schools are plagued by everyday issues, challenges, and nuisances. On any given day, something new surfaces, from a school bus fender bender to students getting back late from a field trip. Given the nature of schools, the amount of people they serve, and their working inner parts, these situations range from the trivial and inconsequential to prominent and dangerous. Since not every situation requires the same degree of action and resources, it is a fundamental skill of school leadership in education to know the difference between a real crisis and another ephemeral complication. We often argue that there should be a class at the graduate level called Firefighter 101: Discerning the Daily Dilemmas from the Consistent Crises in Education. We even tell leaders to ask two questions whenever anything new pops up: Does this need to be solved now? And, does it need to be solved by me?

We like to turn to Covey's quadrants (1989) because they teach us that to effectively manage ourselves and our work, we must focus on the items that are of the utmost importance and that will help us obtain the greatest results. He cautions leaders that we have to be mindful not to fall into the trap of getting caught in a cycle of only working on and solving "urgent" issues that arise throughout the day that prevent us from working on our most "important" areas. That would be the central theme of the Firefighter course, discerning urgent versus important.

It is a vital skill to be able to distinguish the difference between something that is an actual crisis and something that is not.

We subscribe to this philosophy and broaden it, though, to the perennial problems that need extensive focus, collaboration, resources, time, and urgency. Due to the nature of some of our most pressing issues in education, we've almost become numb to how urgent the need is to solve them. As a result, it is a vital skill to be able to distinguish the difference between something that is an actual crisis and something that is not. To do so, we use a simple model that has three basic criteria, shown in Figure 1.1, to determine if an issue is in fact a crisis and should then be dealt with accordingly.

1.1 Model: Important, Urgent, and Persistent

Important

The first criterion determines if the problem is important. One way to determine the importance of an issue is the extent to which it affects student and staff success within the realm of teaching and learning. There are many things throughout the day that are important, but measuring something through the lens of whether or not we are able to achieve our goals is the fulcrum for determining an issue's legitimacy. Schools endorse the power of technology and how it can transform a classroom, but having a highly skilled teacher in front of students is more important than any technological improvement we might make. Therefore, a school leader should exert greater focus, time, and energy finding creative ways to recruit a deeper applicant pool than securing laptops for the 1:1 initiative. This is where diversifying our staff is a crisis and getting a computer in the hands of every student is not. Students can learn without the device; but they can't without the teacher.

Urgent

The second criterion is whether or not the issue is urgent. Urgency is tricky because a juice spill in the hallway can be very urgent if students are in the halls, passing from one class to the other and we're worried that someone might fall. Viewing urgency through a crisis mindset requires us to focus not only on how something should be solved but also who is responsible (Sullivan & Hardy, 2020). A spill in the hallway should not demand the attention of an administrator beyond ensuring that it is being attended to. Don't misunderstand our focus. An all-hands-on-deck approach to running a successful school is needed. But, if an administrator is continually putting out little fires throughout the day, the key drivers of student achievement are not the focus, and the administrator's schedule will only go up in flames.

Persistent

The third criterion is whether or not the issue is persistent. Many urgent and important issues are isolated. They can be solved with a few key decisions and don't have a rippling effect, impacting the function of other aspects of schooling. Throughout this book, we will discuss the mindshifts needed to solve issues along with the right approach to dealing with them. Being perceptive to the depth and breadth of a problem is a skill. Persistent problems are not easily solved, but if our focus is toward the root cause, not the symptom, we stand a chance. Going back to our need for highly skilled teachers, finding creative ways to advertise is a great start, but retaining teachers is one of the most strategic ways to address the teacher shortage problem (Carver-Thomas & Darling-Hammond, 2017). That's one of the primary differences with this new mindshift about recurring problems. In the case that you learn to tell your school's story better to attract new staff, but you can't retain them, the problem persists.

Understanding the crisis mindset model is crucial to begin underscoring the areas of focus for any school to start making serious gains with student achievement. To help teams use the model, we created a Crisis Filter Table so that you can determine where your school will place its attention this year.

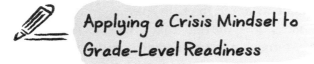

Applying a Crisis Mindset to Grade-Level Readiness

This unfortunate reality in many of our schools of students moving from grade level to grade level without developing the appropriate grade-level skills is a crisis. Whether reading comprehension, mathematical computation, scientific processes or a myriad of other competencies, some students cannot not learn at the required pace in a particular setting. We argue that this is an issue that meets all three of our crisis criteria and does not have an easy solution. Schools struggle with the varying degree of students' ability levels and how to best meet their diverse needs. All the while the school calendar continues to move forward with marking periods beginning and ending and with some students meeting the necessary benchmarks while others fall farther from the pack.

Much of this problem lies at the intersection of time, learning pace, and the scale of the problem in some schools. Although the challenges are numerous, we often look to solve the problems in the context of the classroom period or the typical school day and we may not even see the lost opportunities due to our approach and the way we work to handle the issues.

MAKING THE CONNECTION: GRADE-LEVEL READINESS IN SCHOOLS

As we referenced previously, a lot of students show up to ninth grade and aren't ready to experience the ninth-grade curriculum because of their reading levels. The same is true in sixth grade and fourth grade and every grade level before, thereafter, and in between. It's a perfect example to demonstrate the need for a change and how we've dimmed the light on the problem. Instead, we package similar efforts with different wrapping and hope for better results. We move the system forward regardless of the crises at hand. The path that we've used is so worn that it's the only one to follow. The one we know how.

To make the problem worse, we design a solution that adds to the already overburdened system rather than that changes it. We implement new programs and add time to the students' day when programs and time weren't necessarily getting to the core of what they needed. We can fall into the trap of spending more time on solutions than we do on our analysis of the problem, risking some of our efforts being misguided. It's easy to get stuck in the ways that we've always tackled grade-level readiness by not reflecting on our relationship with it as a problem, a crisis that must be solved.

Unfortunately, we don't have the answers to your grade-level reading problem. There are strategies, programs, and intensive data reviews that can be implemented, but literacy is a crisis that needs a global community effort. It's not just a school issue, but it's a societal issue. Consider schools that have a mobile student population. The number of students who started in the school in kindergarten may be significantly different by the third grade. So the question may be how well do we acclimate new students and parents to the school? How well do we determine their skill levels on day one? Are we able to determine student support in the first week or do we wait to see how they perform? Many of the problems we pose in this book have solutions that you can find with a bit of research, like that of grading that we'll point out in Chapter 2. Grade-level reading is not the case because each school is different. What we do know is that if you're simply adding to the regular school day, especially in ways in which teachers aren't fully trained to implement, the problem isn't being treated with a sustainable plan. We're not getting to the root cause. It could very well be the curriculum. It could be something else, but grade-level reading should be added to your crisis filter, and with three checks, you'll see that it's time to attack it with a mindshift.

 Technical Tip: The Crisis Filter

Successful school leadership teams (SLTs) understand and utilize the process of strategic planning to focus on the most critical areas that lead to the greatest results. Although this is a common activity, too often these plans are narrowly aligned to student achievement results (Bernhardt, 1998). These data are an important metric and because it is quantifiable, it is easier to set clear targets. A deeper look can reveal other conditions and situations directly linked to student achievement.

The table in Figure 1.2 requires teams to participate in an activity that begins with a brain dump of all the pertinent issues and areas of focus being placed in the first column under Area of Focus. We have added some of the common issues that we find in schools. The SLT needs to discuss each one and identify whether or not it is a true crisis using the three-part

1.2 Crisis Filter Table

Area of Focus	Important	Urgent	Persistent	Crisis?
Equity	X	X	X	Yes
Grading Practices	X	X	X	Yes
Third-Grade Reading Levels	X	X	X	Yes
Puke in the Hallway		X		No
Disgruntled Parent	X	X		No
Choose a Reading Month Theme	X		X	No
Staff Shortages	X	X	X	Yes

Crisis Model: Important, Urgent, and Persistent. The lens for each is as follows:

> **Important:** Fundamentally impacts teaching and learning.
> **Urgent:** Time-sensitive, needs immediate attention, and requires skillful resolve.
> **Persistent:** On-going, complex, with long-term implications.

When completing the table, don't hold back on placing issues in the area of focus. Too often, school leaders will omit urgent but small issues because they are common occurrences within the school. Angry parents and spills are common, but ignoring them and not having a system in place to handle them will hijack an administrator's day, preventing her from ensuring that the daily activities are aligned to the strategic focus. So be sure to include a variety of issues you face so you can intentionally develop processes to address them effectively and efficiently.

If an angry parent shows up at school, the administrative assistant should know how to communicate with the parent effectively. If there is a spill in the hall, there should be a clear line of communication to facilities. Both examples are common and can be easily managed, but they are also all too easy to be mishandled and can create unnecessary havoc. The table serves two purposes, one is to identify the limitless number of issues in school; the other is to name what we have as a true crisis.

If an issue meets all three categories, it can be defined as a crisis that needs a mindshift to a crisis mindset that, again, embraces an unfiltered 360° view and approach to solving problems with urgency that abandons conventional wisdom.

In a practical school setting, the model and table are designed to help school leaders concentrate on those elusive and seemingly impossible problems to solve. Let's dig into the teacher shortage issue a bit more. A school's SLT would decide if this is a crisis or not using the three elements in the model. Granted, this is not a crisis for every school system, but we would argue that it is an educational crisis that has been looming for many decades.

The classroom is the most important space in a school. Is the shortage persistent? Yes, since the 1970s fewer and fewer people have been entering the profession. Is it urgent? Yes, each year, more and more classrooms are left without highly qualified teachers at the beginning of the year, particularly in STEM areas. This may not be a crisis within your school system. You may have tons of qualified teachers beating down the doors to get in. That's why every SLT needs to conduct their own analysis. It's also why we don't propose to solve these problems for you. Each school is unique. What we know is that every school needs to make this mindshift if we want these perennial problems to go away.

Reflection Questions

1. What key points stand out to you in this chapter?

2. Does the Crisis Mindset approach run counter to your current thinking about school leadership? If so, how?

3. Think of a current crisis you're addressing—how might a Crisis Mindset approach change the way you're solving that crisis?

4. If you adopted a Crisis Mindset approach, what would change in your leadership practice or strategic planning?

MINDSHIFT #2: LEADING WITH A BATTLEGROUND MENTALITY

In the midst of chaos, there is also opportunity.

—Sun Tzu (2009)

 Outside Story: Lives on the Line

Jocko Willink is a former navy SEAL who consults, writes, and speaks on the topic of leadership. He has a list of central leadership principles, some of which he admits are dichotomous, like his theory that everyone is the same but also different. This leads him to his analogy that great leaders are like master woodworkers—the skills to manipulate the wood are universal, but every piece is uniquely made. Along with his other work, Willink's (2020) *Leadership Strategy and Tactics: Field Manual* speaks to the concept of preparing for battle in business and life the way that SEALs prepare to go to war. It is this idea that inspired our second mindshift, expressed in this chapter, to approach perennial problems with a battleground mentality.

Willink notes that proper preparation in his line of work provides a SEAL with a greater advantage in returning home after a mission and civilians may not experience life or death trials in their roles at work like the military do. Conversely, although he recognizes that civilians don't need SEAL training, he says that everyone can learn from the principles he gathered as a platoon leader even if lives aren't on the line in their profession. We would argue that education does have lives on the line. A quality education, including the more education one has, gives a person an advantage for happiness in life; studies show that it's even more meaningful than income because education and happiness don't have a limit, which has been stressed before in that at a certain point in your financial success, you won't continue to be happier (Striessnig & Lutz, 2016). This means that educators are dealing with the results of our students' lives on a daily basis while they're in school. The more that we can help students see the value of education and the more education they pursue, the happier they'll be. Maybe that's just the kind of "extreme ownership" that Jocko would want us to accept.

What we glean as readers from Willink's work is twofold. First, the military has evolved a great deal from its command-and-control model of leadership to one of explanation and delegation. While still relying a great deal on hierarchy, the troops and their leaders are expected to think collectively about their work and not only value but also depend on teamwork. While many of us have considered the military a place where you learn to do what you're told no matter what you think, Willink goes as far as discussing the reasons why troops might consider a mutiny (he also notes the real consequences in doing so).

Second, Willink cycles back to the concept of detachment. He describes scenarios in which to truly understand the problem, you must remove yourself from it to see the bigger picture, staying grounded but also changing the vantage point. This type of thinking puts the ownership on the soldiers for every aspect of the mission—from understanding the purpose of the work to stepping back and questioning the next moves. It's a relentless style of pushing toward a goal, accepting new ideas, pivoting as needed, and studying the field. We think you'll see this way of attacking problems in what we call a battleground mentality as we define it further in this chapter.

Flawed Thinking: The Educational Industrial Complex

Education in the United States is an industrial complex as powerful as any other global system of domination and control. The system itself poses a threat against freedom and limits opportunities for our already marginalized populations. We hope that you take pause at these last two sentences because we have found that most altruistic educators haven't fully considered the absolute authority that the system has in terms of granting or withholding privilege. Education has the capacity to offer an otherwise disadvantaged youth an opportunity to accumulate wealth beyond that of their parents or grandparents, but the reality is that the system not only thwarts that opportunity but, in many cases, prevents it.

It is with great pain that we point out the damage that is done to the self-esteem, social and emotional well-being, and academic potential of our underserved populations in schools. Despite the rhetoric about narrowing the opportunity gap for students from historically marginalized groups, the gap continues to widen for students of color, and the pandemic only worsened their scripted fate. Sure, there are some schools that have rewritten the script, but they typically have one advantage or another as compared to traditional low-income public systems, and, even then, they're few and far between.

Many fault No Child Left Behind (NCLB), and its regime of test score accountability, as having no greater impact on education than its A Nation at Risk predecessor. Nothing could be further from the truth. No Child Left Behind made a substantial *negative* impression on education, linking for-profit companies, in both theory and cost, to the public sector in a way that had never been done before. Federal stimulus money, pumped into the education arena in 2009, intensified corporate interest in education and, because of new regulations regarding accountability, educators became hungry for strong promises and quick fixes that the system, on its own, could not provide without the new influx of money.

A MARKETPLACE FOR SCHOOLS

First, from a theoretical perspective, No Child Left Behind spawned a dramatic increase in charter schools, often governed as private organizations, including for-profit charters that sought to improve educational opportunities at a lower per-pupil cost than their local government provided so that owners could keep the remaining dollars as profit. These charters also pitted public schools against them, and against each other, in a war to retain current student populations or siphon them off, depending on which side of the battleground you are on. The theory, whether it works or not, is that schools should behave more like the free market whereby high-achieving "profitable" schools will thrive and others will fail and close. The winners in this equation are said to be the children because when their failing schools close, they'll be shifted to a better one. But the reality is that the only shifting that took place as a result of NCLB were resources, which simply became even more unevenly distributed. In many cases, these inequities still exist today.

We don't want to paint the picture as completely grim. The charter school market has benefits for many students. However, it is limited because it can't scale and won't solve problems for the whole education system. Technology, too, along with new programs to support learning, has implications for improving teacher pedagogy. We've witnessed positive shifts in the way that students interact with content, including the data that can be used to make decisions for a differentiated approach to teaching. The concern is that schools that can afford the technology, and the training needed for implementation, are not the ones who need it most. Therefore, the gap that was intended to be closed only widens.

EDUCATORS AS STRATEGIC PLANNERS

To be fair, there is one improvement in education that resulted from NCLB, but certainly not the advent of it—that is the use of strategic planning at the local level of school and district governance. School and district strategic planning didn't make its debut because of NCLB, but schools in America did get more robust planning efforts from it. The concept of strategic planning was bolstered during the NCLB era for many reasons— the school leader was positioned as a businessperson, set to compete with other schools; new funding streams required grants and other lengthy documentation regarding spending; new leadership programming around the country popped up, some with the sole purpose of training corporate and military leaders to become administrators in schools and districts. We did end up with better strategic planning after NCLB, and, for the most part, it has a positive residual effect that may or may not have been calculated by the policy makers from the outset.

Another possible reason why educators became strategic planners during NCLB is because with all the planning documentation needed to garner and use new funding, coupled with the naivety that some educators had about how to plan strategically, companies that help organizations to develop strategic plans suddenly became abundant. If you come upon more money to spend and you need help planning to spend it, it begs the rhetorical question: "why not spend it on planning to spend it?" Then, the plans themselves, claiming to solve current and lasting problems, end up being the reason why the problems won't get solved. The timeline, the process, and the format all end up getting in the way of making change. Spending more money in the public sector ends up being more about spending more money in the public sector than any real reason why we should do so in the first place. Not that strategic planning doesn't have a place or serve a purpose, they just don't work for the crises that exist in schools and that seems to be what we want our strategic plans to attack.

The purpose of a good strategic plan is to determine who will do what by when. These questions are not generally answered in this order, though. The planning usually goes like this: What should we do about X (insert problem) that we're trying to solve? How long will it take us to fix it? And, who should be in charge of making sure that happens? The biggest problem is with the middle question, "how long?" In every attempt to solve huge crises that have burdened the system for ages, we look at 3-, 5-, 10-, and even 15-year planning cycles to get to where we want to be. This is the first of three major problems with strategic planning: *the timeline*. Because of the established timelines in the plans, we've become content with letting our most persistent problems go on even longer. The psychological imprint of the timeline on which the plans unfold provides the planners with the illusion that it's okay to allow problems to fester over time—even indefinitely.

> The psychological imprint of the timeline on which the plans unfold provides the planners with the illusion that it s okay to allow problems to fester over time even indefinitely.

The process used to develop a plan is the second reason why strategic planning doesn't work for perennial problems. Most of the time, an outside agency runs the process. That can be good if the agency is adept at transferring ownership of the plan to the school leaders, but, too often, the plan, developed by the agency, is "owned" by them as the outcome of the process. Sure, the school or district bought the process, which included the final plan. But when the process and the plan are developed by, facilitated by, written by, and delivered by the agency, guess who ends up feeling the closest to the end-product. What schools and districts actually end up with is a story about a plan, not a plan. In other words, the process for developing the plans ends up being more important than the problems that the plans are intended to solve.

Some school leaders might even admit that the story is all that they were looking for in the first place. Because strategic planning includes various stakeholder groups and because all those groups get to provide input into the plan and because there's usually a ton of fanfare during the creation of the plan, we end up with a good story to tell about all of it. That story, and the democratic all-voices-heard process that it follows, often provides a sense of peace that the school or district really does mean business about test scores or school start times, for example. And, we might even get an initiative with a committee out of it—another long program of work with all of our interest groups around the table (that's sarcasm if you didn't sense it).

Yet another reason why strategic planning doesn't work to solve education's persistent problems is because of *the format* in which the final plan typically lives. We don't have to describe these to you—a thick binder, at best it's in the trunk of your car, at worst you have no idea which desk drawer it's in; a persuasive pamphlet, color-coded for the person in the waiting room; a laundry list of data points with targets spread over a thousand years. We could go on. The form in which the goals are displayed is almost never sufficient for true action to be taken by the people who are closest to the problems.

With all of that said, we still believe in the value of a strategic plan and the efforts of bringing together a team to set goals and identify measurements. We just don't want that process to get in the way of how we think about the crises that are currently plaguing our schools and preventing our students from getting the education that they deserve. We don't want the strategic planning endeavor itself to be the reason why the true problems are not identified or why our goals aren't ever met because they're set off on some future date. We don't want to see the education-industrial complex, including for-profit entities, control the way that our communities must respond when we should be, literally, at war with something, anything, that leaves children behind.

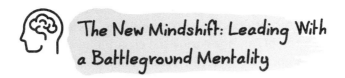

The New Mindshift: Leading With a Battleground Mentality

"When leadership teams wait for consensus before taking action, they usually end up with decisions that are made too late and are mildly disagreeable to everyone. This is a recipe for mediocrity and frustration" (Lencioni, 2012). In his book, *The Advantage*, focused on organizational health, Lencioni goes on to point out that the most effective organizations are not democratic, despite what one might believe about shared decision-making. In education, we have somehow arrived at a theory in practice that decisions, especially those that address problems, should be derived from a process that includes everyone's voice. The failure in this approach is that it implies that everyone will eventually agree with a single best solution to battling perennial problems. That, simply put, is almost never true.

To disassociate with the ineffective consensus approach to problem-solving, we introduce a *Battleground Mentality* as a new way of thinking about age-old issues. The Battleground Mentality requires *a relentless, lives-on-the-line approach where experimentation is used and teams pivot to new ideas in an unapologetic way of constant learning and imple-mentation until a solution is found that works*. This new shift in thinking abandons the notion that every stakeholder will get input when we're solving problems or that any single solution will ever be agreeable to those implementing it. A Battle-ground Mentality assumes that the answers aren't always clear from the start and that we're learning as we're trying new things.

MODEL: RELENTLESS, EXPERIMENTAL, AGILE, AND LEARNING CULTURE

We need to shift our thinking. Organizational psychologist, Adam Grant, says that "requiring proof is an enemy of progress"

(2021). The goal of a learning culture must be to conduct experiments, committing to bets that something might work, and investigating possibilities. In our analysis of the research on how leaders attack a problem to create change, we find four important concepts that must be adopted to reshape our thinking:

R.E.A.L.

1. Relentless: Attack old problems from second-to-second as if in a battle with a fierce enemy. Discard the planning-deliberate-planning cycle.

2. Experimental: Fail faster by implementing more quickly.

3. Agile: Decrease the number of people who provide input.

4. Learning Culture: Shift from a teaching culture to a learning culture where we take risks and learn from mistakes.

R.E.A.L. is the implementation strategy for a Battleground Mentality in that we are going to war against our most troubling and persistent problems with a new way of thinking. In this model, shown in Figure 2.1, leaders become relentless, experimental, and agile within a culture that supports learning over teaching. Let's dissect this further.

2.1 Model: Relentless, Experimental, Agile, and Learning Culture

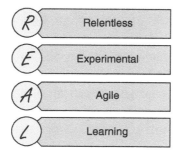

It's not a well-known tidbit about the story of Amazon.com but if you go to relentless.com it will take you directly to their main site. That's because Jeff Bezos originally named the company *Relentless* to signify how persistent he planned to be in creating what we now know as "the everything store." In the early days of the company, when Amazon was an online bookstore, they would literally take orders for books they didn't have, find an obscure bookstore wherever they could, buy the book that their customer requested, and complete the transaction. Today, whether you're in a rural location and you can buy something from Amazon that you would otherwise have to drive miles-and-miles to purchase or you're in an urban setting where you can have something delivered to your door on the same day that you ordered it, Amazon is one of the most influential companies in the world.

> Relentless leaders have an uncompromised focus on what needs to change, and they are fierce about taking swift action.

This type of relentlessness is the first aspect of what it means to shift to having what we call a *Battleground Mentality*. It means that your team is persistent enough to find the things that they don't have and deliver them to the people who need them. It even means that we uncover the needs that people have before they can articulate them. Relentless leaders have an uncompromised focus on what needs to change, and they are fierce about taking swift action. Using a Battleground Mentality, leaders become steadfast to a cause, and their resolve to make things better is often directed at themselves, internally, to prevent every other competing priority of the day from taking their eyes away from the target. It doesn't mean that they're rigid in their thinking; their determination is toward the perennial problem that is so often put on the backburner when so many urgent, yet either unimportant or fleeting, issues arise.

Experimental

Another key shift in adopting a Battleground Mentality is to become far more *experimental*. When we say experimental, we're not just including innovative ideas or the process of design thinking. We expand the definition to include what Rory Sutherland (2019) calls "psycho-logic." Too many of the proposed solutions to our perennial problems in education come from very sound reasoning and logical thinking. But logical reasoning hasn't brought needed results. "While in physics the opposite of a good idea is generally a bad idea, in psychology the opposite of a good idea can be a very good idea indeed" (p. 27). In education, many of our structures and instructional delivery systems are psychological in nature. Consider the concepts of self- and collective efficacy that have been brought to the forefront of what works in schools. Although they are mere psychological phenomena, they work to improve student outcomes, and they deserve experimentation.

We're not talking about experimenting with the way the concrete is poured in the foundation of your school. We leave that to engineers. But how about the way that your teachers start each period of instruction, the way morning meetings are run, and even the way that grades unfold in a unit? We should encourage teachers to run minor experiments from class-to-class or period-to-period to find out which psychological changes yield the best outcomes. Some of these decisions can be based on real data—like the fact that a student's early grades in a new course are strongly correlated to their final score (Jensen & Barron, 2014). Knowing this might prompt a teacher to use a sort of psychological trick at the beginning of every new course or piece of material covered. The impact of doing well early in the course or unit may have something to do with student self-efficacy in the first place and in the long run for their learning. Not that we would make the first graded responses inherently easy, but we do want all students to experience an atmosphere of success in the beginning of the course. It's this type of experimental execution in schools that needs to ramp up so that we can solve our persistent problems faster.

Agile

The "A" in the R.E.A.L. model is a new type of *agile* responsiveness in making change happen with more urgency than we're used to in schools. COVID-19 halted schools, but only at first. After the initial shock, school systems were not only able to make very big changes on the fly, but they pivoted from change-to-change as experiments and new initiatives worked or didn't. It's not just the experimentation that matters but that we move away from what doesn't work and on to something else that might get better results and that we do so quickly.

Consider homework for this example. The role that homework plays in academic gains for students is only partly understood (Trautwein & Köller, 2003). For primary school learners, effects from homework have been said to be right around zero (John Hattie, interview, August 20, 2014), but many teachers (and parents for that matter) demand that we continue to assign it. That's not to say that homework is completely useless, but if it's used as an assignment that penalizes students in the gradebook without proper feedback on their work, the effects can be detrimental. The planning and preparation that goes into homework, the amount of time students spend dreading it and working to complete the task, and the collection, grading, and data entry aspects, coupled with the mystery about whether it works or not, make homework a good contender for something that we might drop so that we can focus on something that might work better.

Perhaps a handful of parents made comments at a track meet about how glad they were that your school still gives homework unlike a neighboring rival school. Reluctancy could be fed if parents rate your school high on some silly app that matters for perception or something like that and cite nightly home-work as a pro. Or, maybe the one year that you announced dropping homework from the curriculum, the parents slaugh-tered you on Facebook, so you'll never do that again. But what about changing it to make it better? How agile are your teachers in the homework arena? Do they know what works and what doesn't? Are they using it for practice or a grade? Is there feedback and self-reflection involved? When was the last time that they tweaked their practice to see if a different approach to homework could produce more effective results in student learning and attitude about school? The problem is that when schools don't know the answers to these questions, they also aren't as agile as they should be. This leads us to the last aspect of a Battleground Mentality that comes from leading through this model of change management, which is shifting from a teaching culture to a learning culture.

Learning Culture

In a teaching culture, teachers are intent to discuss what they do to impart knowledge. This includes planning, delivery, management, and grading. It doesn't always include evidence of what the students actually learned, or, more importantly, what the teacher is trying to learn about students and about how to level up their knowledge of the craft. If you've heard the mantra "It's my job to teach, it's their job to learn," beware you have a teaching culture brewing. What we really want is for everyone to arrive at work as a learner. We call that a *learning culture*.

In a learning culture, the teachers are always focused on their own growth and development. Through professional learning experiences and the review of student outcome data, in a learning culture, everyone is trying to get better for the sake of what students get to experience at school as well as how they do at the tasks we give them. In a learning culture, educators see student assessment data as feedback on their impact and not just the grade that a student earned (Hattie, 2017).

The reason that a shift toward a learning culture in schools is so critical to what it means to adopt a Battleground Mentality is because of how far our profession, and the world of management, has swung toward strength-based feedback. There are huge benefits to the strength-based approach, but Chamorro-Premuzic and Bersin (2018) point out that "In an age where many organizations focus their developmental interventions on 'strengths,' and feel-good approaches to management have substituted 'flaws' and 'weaknesses' with the popular euphemism of 'opportunities,' it is easy to forget the value of negative feedback." They go on to say the following about the development of a true learning culture:

> It is hard to improve on anything when you are unaware of your limitations, fully satisfied with your potential, or unjustifiably pleased with yourself. Although one of the best ways to improve employees' performance is to tell them what they are doing wrong, managers often avoid difficult conversations, so they end up providing more positive than negative feedback. This is particularly problematic when it comes to curiosity and learning, since the best way to trigger curiosity is to highlight a knowledge gap—that is, making people aware of what they don't know, especially if that makes them feel uncomfortable.

We contend that this is the most important distinction for those who seek to switch their school culture to that of one that values learning over teaching—we consistently work toward an understanding of our limitations and the ways that we can address them. It means that we're more often uncomfortable than comfortable.

Using the R.E.A.L. model of problem-solving to adopt a Battleground Mentality is easier said than done. It's hard to stay relentless on solving big problems with everything else going on day-to-day; it's distressing to experiment when we want to use current practices and logical reasoning in our planning; it's difficult to let go, moving quickly without consensus, gathering input from fewer people before making a significant change; and, it's uncomfortable to be part of a learning culture that focuses on what we don't know versus what we do know. To adopt the R.E.A.L. model for battle-ground thinking means that school leaders make a mindshift and take on a completely different way of thinking and leading than what we are used to. We want to acknowledge how demanding that can be. We also assert that not doing so will leave you grappling with the same old issues that your institution faces year-over-year. Finding new ways of thinking about old problems is a choice.

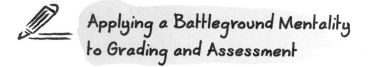

Applying a Battleground Mentality to Grading and Assessment

"If you want to start an argument about some aspect of education, you need only bring up the way teachers grade" (Guskey & Brookhart, 2019, p. 1). Grading and assessment may in fact be the most controversial teaching and learning practice that we have in education. We can't think of another subject of education reform with so much personal bias infused into the conversation and so much variance in practice between one teacher and another. Unless schools or systems have truly adopted a research-based standards-driven approach to grading, it's likely still the wild, wild, west of determining a student's outcome on a report card for parents.

What these passionate debates fail to recognize is that grading is an equity issue, among other concerns regarding what a grade really means and how it communicates success in school or not. What we know for sure is that the students who suffer the most from teachers' variance and variability in grading practices are our already marginalized student populations (Feldman, 2019). "Fixing" grading has implications for helping students to learn and to see school as a safe place. Instead of seeing grades as their ultimate demise, using multiple attempts and other revision strategies—a practice not widely used in today's schools—students might otherwise build confidence and self-efficacy rather than break it down.

We also know that grading reform and certain practices in particular—like the aforementioned use of a redo or retake policy—are based on research not conjecture. Guskey and Brookhart (2019) point out that too many of our grading practices are derived from opinions about what works and not the deep well of information that can be accessed as it relates to the studies that have been conducted on the subject. Instead of reaching for the proof of what works, we argue using our experiences as educators, some of which date back as far as what was done to us in school.

School leaders need not go very far to find the crisis at hand. A grade book audit at many schools will show that, in general, Black students are more likely to receive Ds or Fs than their white counterparts. An audit of this type might also show that the same two courses, taught by different teachers, have vastly different assignments and even different grading scales and criteria for success. Equity concerns coupled with curriculum inaccuracies alone make grading a battleground. It's the reason why we need a new way to think about this old problem.

MAKING THE CONNECTION: GRADING AND ASSESSMENT IN SCHOOLS

Let's apply the R.E.A.L. model to improve the efficacy of grading and assessment practices. First, you need to be relentless about grading practices. It has to be something that comes up on just about every meeting agenda, every walkthrough, every PLC, and every teacher observation. Every single staff member knows that your intent on changing the system in a deep and meaningful way. Your most ardent supporters know and so do your strongest resisters. The minute you let your foot off the pedal is the minute that others see that you've relented, allowing old habits to persist because the change agent isn't completely consistent.

For grading to transform, we also need to engage with new and different experiments in terms of how we assess and assign grades. This is where the concept of your first followers comes into play. You only need one or two people to commit at first, or perhaps an entire grade level or department is willing to play around with new ideas. We often hear leaders talk about the desire to have a culture where risk-taking is a norm. What we really want is a *culture of try*. We want teachers to try something new—test it out, reflect, and refine. This book isn't about what to change but how to get change to occur. As such, we suggest that you reach for *Assessing With Respect* (2021) by Starr Sackstein, and other books of its kind, to learn what you might try as an experiment. You just need to get folks to make small changes that will lead to bigger modifications as well as permanent changes, which eventually permeate the staff as the first followers begin to multiply.

Third, as experiments fail, the team needs to be *agile*, willing to tweak what we're doing on the fly. When the first followers are meeting about an aspect of grading that they changed but that doesn't appear to be functioning the way it should, the answer can't be to go back to the old practice, which is unfortunately the case when a change isn't sticky yet. Instead, the group needs to adjust, adopting an additional variation, pushing the innovation further rather than snapping back to the old ways. We have to be careful when we experiment because, in a that-didn't-work culture, the instinct is typically to revert back to old habits when the new strategy doesn't produce the desired results. Agility requires us to stay within a confused and unsure state until the modifications we're making bring us into a condition of renewal.

Finally, we have to foster a *learning culture* when it comes to grading or any other change that requires educators to learn new skills, adopt new theories of action, or understand complex problems as they are. Learning cultures move faster because they never consider a current practice or present structure to be without substitution or analysis. In true learning cultures, every actor not only calls into question the practices in use but also their own thoughts and behaviors. Instead of the threat of embarrassment of not being certain about the correct approach to the craft, there's a threat of embarrassment in not being open to seeing things differently and making a change.

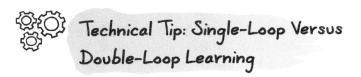

Technical Tip: Single-Loop Versus Double-Loop Learning

A lot of the research that we've done regarding organizational learning comes from the work of Chris Argyris. Argyris coined the terms "single-loop" and "double-loop" learning to demonstrate the difference between working to solve a problem and continuous improvement. The distinction is that problem-solving is about preventing error while continuous improvement is about learning from failure and achieving longer-term goals.

Consider the example that Argyris uses in his book, *On Organizational Learning* (1992).

> A thermostat that automatically turns on the heat whenever the temperature in a room drops below 68° is a good example of single-loop learning. A thermostat that could ask, "Why am I set at 68°?" and then explore whether or not some other temperature might more economically achieve the goal of heating the room would be engaging in double-loop learning. (p. 127)

The analogy demonstrates a higher degree of thinking about problems. It's the reasoning needed to solve perennial problems in education as well. Double-loop learning analyzes the situation from an end-goal standpoint rather than short-term fix. Going back to grading as our example in this chapter, instead of using grades as a motivational tactic to get students to complete work, we would need to completely shift the thinking more toward using grading as a tool to assess learning to be able to provide feedback or adjust a lesson. The former is the equivalent of heating the room (the room needs heating; the work needs to get done). The latter, on the other hand, is akin to figuring out the best adjustment to make to reach the ultimate goal—student learning.

Schools ought to use a double-loop learning approach to develop a learning culture so that we're responding to problems as learners. The alternative, unfortunately what many schools endure, is a lack of systemic analysis regarding problems that have been around for ages. We respond the way that we know how versus using a new strategy regardless of the fact that it might bring new problems or even failure.

Reflection Questions

1. Consider one of your school's perennial problems. What impact could a Battleground Mentality have on that crisis?

2. What part of the R.E.A.L. model would be most important for your school to implement? Why?

3. What part of the R.E.A.L. model would be most challenging for your school to implement? Why?

4. What are some action steps that you can take to move your school closer to a learning culture?

MINDSHIFT #3: LEADING WITH A BEGINNER'S MIND

If your mind is empty, it is always ready for anything, it is open to everything.

—Shunryu Suzuki (2010)

We would like to dedicate this chapter to Harvard Professor Richard Elmore. His last public discussion of education was on TheSchoolhouse302 Podcast, The One Thing Series School Leadership Podcast, and he referenced a Beginner's Mind as the key to learning and solving problems in the field of education.

 Outside Story: This Should Exist

Sara Blakey was a door-to-door fax machine salesperson who never took a single business class in college, never worked in retail, and had zero experience in the fashion industry. Yet, her willingness to try something and fix an issue with a product she used regularly led to a new category in women's hosiery. Sara Blakey is the founder and owner of the shape-wear brand Spanx, and her inexperience might be what led to her colossal success.

It all started with a pair of cream pants. Blakey refused to concede to wearing painful undergarments just to look and feel good in her favorite pants. Her nylons hid pantylines, kept her hips and thighs smooth and tight, but covered her feet—including her toes. She wanted to wear a pair of open-toed shoes to a Florida event, but Blakey knew that even though wearing her pantyhose would make her body appear firmer, they would show a nylon seam on her toes—a fashion faux-pas. What did she do? She cut off the feet from a pair of pantyhose. Her thought was that it would keep her cooler, allow her to look her best, and show off her pedicure. At the end of the day, she was generally satisfied with how she looked and was initially willing to accept the hassle of her nylons rolling up from her ankles. Then, she thought, *why live with the discomfort; there has to be a product that keeps wearers looking shapely without the annoyance of the pantyhose rolling up.*

So her journey began. In her quest to deliver a product that would make women look good without discomfort, Blakey discovered that most pantyhose were made by people not wearing them. Sara's naiveness gave her the freedom to tackle problems that more experienced companies overlooked or accepted as unavoidable. For example, as Blakey began her research to develop footless hosiery, she discovered that every size of pantyhose had the same size waistband. Small and large women were expected to make it work. To Blakey, this was ridiculous. Why hadn't anybody questioned the size of the tiny rubber cord that held the hose in place?

Sara's lack of business sense, but clear vision, unbridled her innovation, which wasn't confined by the industry norm but rather what's best for women. She focused on her experience as a consumer and posed questions like: Do the pantyhose stay in place? How long do they hold up? Are they comfortable? Do you feel good in them? Prototypes were tried on actual women, not the plastic forms that the hosiery mills used for their products. Blakey rejected the belief that discomfort was something women just had to endure if they wanted to look good.

Her willingness to fix and take on a common problem for women didn't come from extensive knowledge of pantyhose or the fashion industry but rather unrestricted thinking that was poised to serve women. Blakey proved that sometimes a Beginner's Mind—a willingness to suspend prior ideas, knowledge, and experience—can produce superior results.

Flawed Thinking: The Expert Blind Spot

Remember the professor who was filled with knowledge in their subject area, possibly brilliant, but you just couldn't follow the lecture? Perhaps you've been in classrooms where the teacher is passionate about the content, but loses students when making connections to related ideas. This is what is known as an *expert blind spot*. It refers to the inability to interact with information as if it's completely new and fresh. It accepts experience and knowledge as a given and fails to rethink, question, or reimagine what we believe to be true.

WHAT YOU KNOW CAN HURT YOU

It might seem unbelievable that our expertise could actually interfere with our ability to solve problems. Abraham Luchins (1942) a German psychologist, conducted a famous study called *The Water Jug Experiment*. The study was designed to investigate mental flexibility in thinking. In other words, if people can successfully solve a problem one way, can they shift their problem-solving process when faced with similar, but different, problems? Could people identify new, simpler, and more efficient ways of solving a problem or does their previous knowledge create mental rigidity in their thinking?

The experiment worked like this: participants in the experimental group were given five practice problems that could be solved by decoding a common formula. The goal was to use the given capacities of three different jars to obtain a desired amount of water. The chart in Figure 3.1 shows the units that each jug held and the desired quantity that could be achieved using the solution: B minus A minus 2 times C. In Problem 2, the goal was to get 100 units in the jar. This could be done by starting with 127 units in Jar B, then removing 21 units using Jar A and 6 units using Jar C twice. Note, the control group was not provided with these practice questions.

Then, both groups were given critical Problems 6 through 10, shown in Figure 3.2. While the critical problems 6-9 could be solved using the same formula in the first five problems, there was always a simpler solution. Not only did most of the participants from the first group continue to apply a lengthier method to achieve the desired capacity, but they were also unsuccessful in finding a solution to Problem 10, which could not be solved using the previous formula. The control group, who were not given the first five practice problems, were able to find the most efficient method for solving the critical problems as well as the solution to the tenth problem.

3.1 The Water Jug Experiment Practice Problems

Problem #	Jar A Capacity	Jar B Capacity	Jar C Capacity	Desired Capacity
1	21	127	3	100
2	14	163	25	99
3	18	43	10	5
4	9	42	6	21
5	20	59	4	31

3.2 The Water Jug Experiment Critical Problems

Problem #	Jar A Capacity	Jar B Capacity	Jar C Capacity	Desired Capacity
6	23	49	3	20
7	15	39	3	18
8	28	76	3	25
9	18	48	4	22
10	14	36	8	6

The results of his study show that once people experience success solving a problem one way, they tend to continue solving it the same way even if the approach is less efficient or doesn't work at all. The experiment revealed what is now known as *The Einstellung effect*. It showed that original success tethered participants; they failed to explore better, even simpler, solutions to additional problems in the future (Luchins, 1942). Our past experience and memory create a path of least resistance; we rely on it rather than experimenting and exerting more cognitive energy to create new solutions. Our perception is that we already have *the* solution. Our experience leaves us oblivious to potential better solutions because our brains are applying a cognitive bias or expert blind spot.

OVER RELYING ON EXPERTISE

For those who consider themselves as nonexperts, trying to keep up with the thinking of someone who exudes confidence in their knowledge is intimidating. Edujargon, presumptions about shared experiences, and assumptions of prior knowledge can alienate others in group settings. While knowledge and understanding are crucial to teaching and learning, they are not the sole determiner of success in the classroom. Indeed, the amount of content knowledge a teacher has is not as influential on student learning as most people assume it is.

Researcher, professor, and author John Hattie synthesized five meta-analyses from 151 studies to determine that teacher subject matter knowledge has an effect size of only 0.19. Even though it is true that 0.19 is still a positive impact, it is significantly below the 0.40 hinge point or average of all other influences on student learning. Hattie categorizes effect sizes between 0.15 and 0.40 as what we can expect in a typical year of school. Teacher subject knowledge falls in the lower range of this zone and is not likely to accelerate student learning (Hattie, 2009).

However, Cognitive Task Analysis (CTA), which is a cluster of research methods to uncover the thinking process that experts use and access the way they interpret problems, how they interact with them, and, ultimately, how they strategize to solve them, has a much larger effect size (Clark, Feldon, Van Merrienboer, Yates, & Early, 2008). The CTA process reveals what experts do or think intuitively as problem-solvers. Experts are guided in a way that acknowledges the steps that were taken, what they noticed, and goals they instinctively established that novices might miss. It effectively slows down the cognitive process so that there are no assumptions made about what, why, or how an expert is thinking about a problem.

With an effect size of 1.29, CTA has the potential to considerably accelerate student learning (Hattie, 2021). This metacognitive effort to identify thought processes can also expose bias that an expert might have, which is preventing them from seeing other opportunities. In short, CTA forces experts to reflect on their thinking and actions using a Beginner's Mind to expose blind spots.

EXPOSING BLIND SPOTS

In their book, *Curiosity Muscle*, Andy Fromm and Diana Kander (2018) offer a four-step framework to keep curiosity alive and prevent what we already know from interfering with what more we could learn or discover.

What are the blind spots? Not only can we be unaware of the limitations that our experiences create, but our bias also thrives in our overconfidence in our knowledge level as well. *Confirmation bias* is when we seek affirmation for our preconceived beliefs. This happens through selective listening and superficial questions, designed to lead others or conversations to support what we already think is true. Overconfidence, bias, and gut feelings about what will or won't work creates blinders to potential solutions.

Are you focused on the right things? When we put too much faith in our expertise, our ability to reflect on our programs, policies, and processes diminishes. *Attention bias* is "the tendency to prioritize the processing of certain types of stimuli over others" (Azriel & Bar-Haim, 2020). The focus shifts to aspects of perennial problems that may not lead to the type of change needed to prevent these educational crises from popping up over and over. For example, summarizing an overall gain in student achievement, but ignoring a widened gap in the success of students with low socioeconomic status within the reported gains.

What can you test? Too often educators choose not to take any action at all because there is not a 100 percent guarantee that our efforts will be successful. In a crisis, there is a greater willingness to try something—anything, then assess what worked and what didn't, make modifications, and keep going with iterations until a reasonable solution is reached. Unfortunately, with stagnant problems such as teacher retention, equity, inclusion, and social and emotional learning, that same level of urgency to take action is not always present. This leads to a delayed response under the premise that we aren't sure that any of the potential solutions will work.

How can we engage others to help solve this problem? Having the right people at the table is the first step in looking for potential answers to old lingering problems. Avoid excluding or dismissing individuals because they might not understand a particular situation or the intricacies of how a school is run. Fresh minds can be valuable in offering a perspective that those in the trenches might overlook. More experts are not always how we find the answer.

By purposefully walking through these types of questions, we call attention to the possibility of an expert blind spot. This gives us the opportunity to expose cognitive or confirmation bias explicitly. In *The Water Jug Experiment*, when the experimental group was given a cue to heighten their awareness, over half of them shifted their thinking and adjusted to the simpler solution (Luchins & Luchins, 1959). Being aware of expert blind spots gives us a chance to unveil our cognitive, confirmation, and/or attention bias when attempting to develop new solutions to old problems. This is why we offer the next new mindshift and invite you to Lead With a Beginner's Mind.

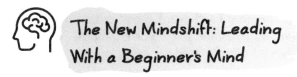

The New Mindshift: Leading With a Beginner's Mind

A *Beginner's Mind* comes from a Zen Buddhism concept called Shoshin, which *is an attitude of openness, eagerness, and lack of preconceptions that leads to greater understanding.* This mindshift enables us to rethink our "expert" view on educational problems, encouraging us to see issues through a new lens so that our expertise or experience isn't a hindrance. Shunryu Suzuki, a Sōtō Zen monk who is largely credited with bringing Buddhism to the United States said, "In the beginner's mind, there are many possibilities, in the expert's mind there are few." This means that there are occasions when experience is the enemy of innovation.

The longer we see an issue one way, the harder it is to change our thinking about that issue. And, the longer a problem persists, the more likely it is accepted as unsolvable. These are the very issues we claim are becoming silent crises in education. Teacher burn-out, inequity, student dropouts, violence in schools, and apathy toward learning are issues nearly every school faces and cannot solve. Instead of applying an old mindset to a persistent problem, let's position ourselves as novices or amateurs, abandoning the experience and expertise we have that hasn't been able to solve this ongoing problem.

Let's look at a population of natural questioners: children. They progress through their development where nearly everything is new to them. This makes them inquisitive. Their organic curiosity is born from a beginner's mindset. If you've ever been around a preschooler who has perfected the series of "why" questions, you know the multitude of questions these inquirers ask. The ability for children to ask so many questions results from a series of complex mental maneuvers (Harris, 2012). First, they have to have the metacognition to recognize when they don't know something. Additionally, children have to understand that there are multiple possible responses to their question. Harris (2012) writes, "Without the ability to conceive of more than one possible way that things might stand in the world, why ask a question?" Finally, children have found a source that helps them get answers to their inquiries—they ask someone who they believe will know. These three mentalities keep them curious and don't allow them to accept that they know something for sure.

MENTALITIES FOR A BEGINNER'S MIND

1. I don't know the solution to this problem.
2. There are multiple solutions to this problem.
3. I will consult with someone who has expertise.

MODEL: DISCOVER, COLLECT, PROCESS, AND RESPOND

There are four characteristics included in our model for Leading with a Beginner's Mind. Each of the traits, shown in Figure 3.3, focuses on a specific aspect of how this mindshift should interact with information. They address how leaders

3.3 Model: Discover, Collect, Process, and Respond

Discover Information	Collect Information	Process Information	Respond to Information
Employ a Playful Mind	Attend Like a Novice	Forget What You Think You Know	Avoid Certain Actions and Behaviors

who implore a Beginner's Mind to discover, collect, process, and respond to information.

Discover Information

The playful mind impacts our ability to discover information. This trait, which we call *Employ a Playful Mind*, is the first of four characteristics included in our model for a Beginner's Mind. In the classroom, we ask students to think like a historian or write like an author. The same idea can be applied to adults when looking to trigger a specific thinking perspective. The playful mind creates avenues of thinking not readily tapped into by adults. When our creative juices are flowing, innovative solutions are more likely to surface. We can discover ideas that we may not have recognized without employing a playful mind.

Collect Information

Shoshin encourages the release of presumptions and embraces an attitude of openness as if you're experiencing information for the first time. Whether consciously or unconsciously, the more knowledge we have on a topic, we naturally don't give it the attention it may deserve. Perhaps it's a sense of confidence, or *over*confidence, that sparks an "I already know this" attitude which causes our attention to wane, but it should work in the opposite way. The more information that you have about a given topic, the more closely you should pay attention to uncover what you may be missing. This is the second trait of a Beginner's Mind, and it calls for thinkers to **Attend Like a Novice**. When we find ourselves losing focus, dismissing ideas, or not wanting to collect additional data and information, we have to humble ourselves and concentrate on the Shoshin principle to collect information as if we know nothing about it.

The more information that you have about a given topic, the more closely you should pay attention to uncover what you may be missing.

Process Information

As demonstrated in the *Water Jug Experiment*, our brains can actually block us from processing information and solving problems in better ways when solutions exist. It doesn't matter if they are inefficient or ineffective, the brain won't cooperate. This brings us to the third characteristic of the Beginner's Mind model which is **Forget What You Think You Know**. In order to eliminate expert blind spots, we have to consciously free our minds from preconceived beliefs when processing new information. Maintaining a mentality that a better solution exists, whether discovered yet or not, will prevent limiting thoughts and ideas from creeping in and sabotaging progress.

RESPOND TO INFORMATION

When trying to avoid the Einstellung effect, we must be cognizant of our words and actions. To respond with a Beginner's Mind, James Clear (2018), author of *Atomic Habits*, suggests that we can behave as Shoshin instructs by letting go of certain actions. The six behaviors that undermine a Beginner's Mind are the need to add value, the need to win every argument, dominating conversations, saying "I know," having a fixed mindset, and holding prejudices and labels (see Figure 3.4 *Respond with a Beginner's Mind*). This call to *Avoid Certain Actions and Behaviors* makes up the final key component of our Beginner's Mind model.

3.4 Respond With a Beginner's Mind

Avoid	Beginner's Mind Trait	Example
Need to Add Value	Allow others to share their experiences	Giving unsolicited advice or sharing your own successes when others are talking about their experiences refocuses the energy on what we think we already know rather than seeking to gain more understanding about what the other person is sharing.
Need to Win Every Argument	Consider alternate points of view	Look at alternate viewpoints from the perspective of "Isn't that an interesting perspective?" Even if someone is wrong, you don't have to point it out every time.
Dominating Conversations	Listen more, talk less	If you're talking, you're not listening. Try asking someone to "tell me more about that" to encourage others to have the floor.

3.4 (Continued)

Avoid	Beginner's Mind Trait	Example
"I Know"	Pretend you're learning for the first time	Approach discussions with an assumption that you're an idiot. Even if you think you know something, refrain from telling everyone.
Fixed Mindset	Growth Mindset	A growth mindset encourages curiosity and sees failure as an opportunity to learn and improve.
Prejudices and Labels	Unbiased thinking	Compartmentalizing can lead to prejudice. Labels encourage our preconceived notions to be accepted as truth without challenging them. Keep an open mind where you express humility. Humans are built to categorize information; we have to evade it to see things from another perspective.

Source: Adapted from James Clear, 2018.

When leaders are applying a Beginner's Mind, they mindfully use these characteristics so they can discover, collect, process, and respond to information with a new perspective. It is a mindshift that balances knowledge and experience without being immobilized by an expert blind spot.

BUILDING A SPAGHETTI AND MARSHMALLOW TOWER

We think it is no coincidence that the most learning occurs between the ages of four and twelve (Janacsek, Fiser, & Nemeth, 2012). Children have fewer life experiences to lead (or should we say impede) their thinking. They innocently pose questions for the sole purpose of building understanding. Prior learning doesn't obstruct new learning. Tom Wujec (2010) conducted a famous activity called the Marshmallow Challenge. The results suggest that it isn't simply lack of knowledge that allows a Beginner's Mind to flourish, it's the novice status and the willingness to implement ideas that produce success.

In the Marshmallow challenge, teams are given twenty sticks of raw spaghetti, one yard of tape, one yard of string, and one marshmallow. They are tasked with producing the tallest

3.5 Spaghetti and Marshmallow Tower

Source: FFM Tooth Pick (2008) by Warburg https://commons.wikimedi a.org/wiki/File:FFM_tooth-pick.JPG CC BY-SA 3.0

freestanding structure that they can in eighteen minutes. Examples of structures are shown in Figure 3.5. Business school students performed the worst with an average height of about ten inches. Lawyers were not much better with a structure that stood at fifteen inches. Among the best performing groups were kindergarteners. Their structures averaged twenty-six inches tall. Wujec (2010) credits the success of the five-year-olds with their willingness to iterate. They had no preconceived notions about what would or would not work, so they started with the marshmallow and built prototypes, improving on their model with multiple structures. Business students, on the other hand, are conditioned to anticipate a single correct answer. They spent most of their time applying logic and sharing information they could contribute, eventually running out of time before they could put it to the test. They believed they could figure out the answer based on their collective knowledge rather than seeking evidence of what works and improve from there.

For educators to apply this same process, we first have to cognitively accept that we might not have a solution—or even a nonsolution, something we can rule out because it's not effective. If we can embrace this truth, we then have to consciously open our thinking to other possibilities. The Einstellung effect makes this more challenging for adults because our experiences guide us. This isn't to suggest that past experience can't be useful; however, we have to be aware that the more successful events we have, the less inclined we are to seek better solutions. We should be mindful of this trap when working to solve problems that seem impossible. Instead of trying to retrieve information that we believe we already hold, we need to force our minds to be flexible and consider new ways of thinking.

THINK YOUNG

Unfortunately, we don't have a time machine to go back to our youth to maximize our creative capacity and solve today's problems. We do have the ability to consciously permit our minds to think more openly—more like children. More mature minds tend to be rule following, goal setting, and, over time, stifle novel thinking. We will call this adult tendency a *solution-mind.* Young brains not only have fewer experiences from which to draw, but they tend to be more impulsive. Their frontal cortex, where self-control and rule-based behavior is controlled, develops slower than other parts of the brain. Their natural sense of following a protocol is not as prevalent in children as it is in adults. The adult, solution-mind, needs to shift when working to find solutions to problems, and employ the *playful mind* of children, since they are more likely to see a task as an opportunity to engage in play.

Thankfully, mindsets are flexible; it is not impossible to encourage a solution-mind to think more playfully. In their study, Zabelina and Robinson (2010) asked 76 college students what they would do if school was canceled for the day. One group was asked to imagine themselves as seven-year-olds. The group of adults who were prompted to *think young* produced more original responses, showing more creativity in their thinking using the Torrance Test of Creative Thinking. Simply triggering adults to shift their thinking to being more child-like allowed them to think more freely. The impact on more reserved and inhibited participants was even greater.

Triggering a playful mind to find solutions to deep-rooted problems is one way to maximize the brain power of those you lead. It isn't that we want educators to forget everything they know, but we do have to unlock the limitations that solution-minds hold onto that prevent out-of-the-box thinking. Fortunately, it is possible to embrace a new way of thinking and working toward meaningful solutions.

While it might seem simple to execute this mindshift, be careful—that may be your expert blind spot kicking in. Recognize that Leading with a Beginner's Mind requires a concerted effort and awareness of our own limitations and a willingness to view situations, old or new, with a fresh look. The more we know, the greater potential for flawed thinking unless we intentionally make this mindshift. As Claude Bernard, a famous physiologist from the 1800s, said, "It is what we know already that often prevents us from learning."

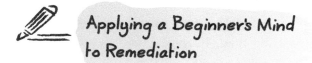
Applying a Beginner's Mind to Remediation

Whether it's through multitiered systems of supports, response to intervention (RTI), inclusion or remediation, every school has students who require something more than quality instruction to become proficient in the core curriculum. Mounds of research, excessive professional development, piles of resources, and hours of team meetings have been dedicated to solving this everlasting problem. Millions of grant dollars have been spent on services and tools for students who are not performing as well as their grade-level peers. Yet, this perennial ghost of underperformance continues to accept flawed thinking, leading to inconsistent results at best. A leader with a Beginner's Mind can change that.

MAKING THE CONNECTION: STUDENT REMEDIATION IN SCHOOLS

A common process used to determine which students need additional supports includes reviewing data from standardized, benchmark, and formative assessments. Once students are identified as not meeting expectations, a plan is developed and executed for filling in the gaps, hoping these students will somehow "catch-up" to their grade-level peers. Nevertheless, even with support, many students remain designated as "at-risk," "struggling," or "low." Some never close the gap and for others, the gap widens. Yet, the way most systems address their needs is reactive—wait for students to underperform or worse yet, fail, then double-up instruction to fill the academic voids.

Perhaps it's an expert blind spot that has some educators clinging to the idea of retention, believing that when students repeat what they missed, they will master the grade-level skills. We can all think of a student in our career who, after repeating a grade in elementary school, blossomed and went on to be top of the class on graduation day. That single success story can influence our thinking to advocate that more students should be held back so they can experience a year of learning for the second time. However, the research is clear. Students who are retained are much more likely to be pushed out before earning a diploma (Hughes et al., 2018). In fact, the effect size of 255 research studies on the impact of retention was calculated at −0.32 (Hattie, 2021). Retention, overall, reverses the impact of learning.

Student retention is the ultimate remediation strategy. Less extreme remediation tactics like response to intervention, extra classroom support, intervention time, or study clubs are strategies schools use to assist students who, the data reveal, are being failed by the system. The expert mind, by design, focuses on strategies and programs that can assist students who are on the list of unsuccessful learners. This reactive approach puts students on a schedule to spend time and cognitive energy trying to pick up what wasn't learned the first time around while trying to keep up with the new learning. This cycle rarely works. Too often they fall farther and farther behind unit-by-unit, month-by-month, and grade-by-grade.

A Beginner's Mind brings a different approach. Rather than doubling down on the same methods, just at different times or in different classrooms, the support for these students looks different. Rather than remediating learning that didn't stick the first time, why not front-load information in place of back-tracking? This is precisely the question Justin Minkel asked (2015).

> Remediation is often a terrible way to help kids catch up. Pre-teaching is more effective and more fun ... For the same 20-minutes investment of time, we can change the way a child sees himself (sic) as a reader, thinker, or mathematician. We can give Manuel the rare experience of being the kid who gets it first, who helps the other kids figure it out, who is ready with the answer the moment he hears the question. (Minkel, 2015)

Mr. Minkel is an elementary teacher in Springdale, Arkansas, whose beginner's mind about remediation brought him to use preteaching as an intervention. At the time, his approach was unconventional and caught the attention of researcher Ruth Trundley. Trundley set out to see how Minkel's theory played out in mathematics. Her project confirmed that not only did student competence improve, but several other benefits surfaced. Student self-efficacy improved, engagement during the lesson increased, students asked more challenging questions, learners served as learning mentors to other students, and the overall attitude toward mathematics was more positive (Trundley, 2018).

This example of how dismantling the flawed thinking of re-teaching and dissecting the needs from a fresh perspective provided positive results and research for a practice that is now proven to be effective in math. Richard Elmore (2002) explained it this way: "Unexamined wallpaper is classroom practices and institutional policies that are so entrenched in school culture or a teacher's paradigm that their ability to affect student learning is never probed." We interpret this to mean that sometimes solutions are right in front of us, but we are so distracted by what we already think we know that we don't question methods that should be questioned.

> *Sometimes solutions are right in front of us, but we are so distracted by what we already think we know that we don't question the methods that should be questioned.*

Students needing additional support beyond what quality instruction can offer is an ongoing problem in American schools. A Beginner's Mind considers multiple options for improved success. Rather than trying to solve the problem through more teaching, it considers the learner. It lets go of the assumption that how we previously achieved success is the only option for future success. It invites curiosity, questioning, and healthy criticism when results are insufficient. Embracing a mindshift to a Beginner's Mind can explore innovative solutions, not just for remediation, but for any persistent problem in education.

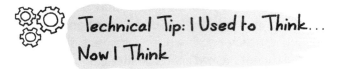

Technical Tip: I Used to Think... Now I Think

There are countless ways to effectively close a lesson. Many teachers use exit tickets to formatively assess student mastery of a learning target, essentially, by measuring content learning. Activities such as this provide both teachers and students evidence on the success of a lesson and determine next steps to build on that learning. Now and again, lesson closure may have more of a metacognitive purpose. Reflection is encouraged so that learners can think about their thinking. These prompts determine what was difficult, how they tackled a problem, what strategies were helpful, or their mindset and disposition toward the content.

An effective strategy to spark metacognition and spotlight how thinking changes as learning develops is a strategy out of the Visible Thinking work at Project Zero, Harvard Graduate School of Education. It's called *I Used to Think... Now I Think*. The purpose of the protocol is to emphasize new under-standings, changed opinions, and what new thinking they have gained as a result of a lesson.

Applying the *I Used to Think... Now I Think* method when faced with educational crises can offer benefits for those engaging in the activity. First, asking problem-solvers to label how their thinking has changed leads with the expectation that it has, indeed, changed. There is an inherent belief that through thought and dialogue our opinions and understanding are likely to shift. Labeling initial thinking and connecting it to new thinking invites a Beginner's Mind. It signifies that we can and have changed our minds. Second, it calls attention to what might have caused a change in thinking. In order to expose expert blind spots, we analyze our thought processes which reveal how we are able to get a fresh perspective and attempt to see problems from a naiver viewpoint. It tells us *why* we have changed our minds.

Richard Elmore constantly challenged us to look at schools, instruction, and learning from a Beginner's Mind. Despite his vast knowledge and experience, he strived to maintain a perspective that was absent from bias so that he could optimize his own learning. His commitment to keeping receptive thinking is evidenced by his book *I Used to Think...* *And Now I Think*. In the book, leading educators, considered to be experts at every level of school reform, detail how their Beginner's Mind challenged and influenced their thinking. Elmore compiles their reflections and invites readers to learn how the book's contributors followed the concept of Shoshin.

One modification to the *I Used to Think... Now I Think* protocol is to start it before the problem-solving process begins. Encourage decision-makers to share their current thinking. Document it. Then, as the problem-solving process flows, circle back to initial thoughts to see if and how they have changed. Setting your sessions up in this way provides a visual reminder of assumptions and beliefs that were once held by individuals and your group. It also brings a third point of reference so that as outlooks morph, they are detached from individuals in the group. It might be easier for team members to let go of an idea if it's already been categorized as how they "used to think."

Reflection Questions

1. How are blind spots working as obstacles in your current work? What areas can you identify that would benefit from a Beginner's Mind?

2. Think of a time when you had an expert blind spot. What will you do in the future to open your thinking to diverse perspectives?

3. What type of resistance could you anticipate if you approach a problem with a Beginner's Mind? How can that resistance be resolved?

4. How might a mindshift to a Beginner's Mind impact your role as a leader?

MINDSHIFT #4:
LEADING WITH AN
OCTOPUS APPROACH

A system is never the sum of its parts, it's the product of their interaction.

—Russell Ackoff (2003)

Outside Story: A Boundaryless Organization

Longtime CEO of General Electric and leadership guru Jack Welch used to ask, "What's the reality?" at his team meetings. He truly wanted to know how each element within the companies that comprised General Electric was performing. He demanded a candid, raw, evaluation of every aspect of the organization. Under Welch, General Electric's value soared from $14 to $410 billion, while revenue increased to $105 billion (Bostock, 2020). He never underestimated the problems, strived for simplicity, and worked to ensure that the organization, although composed of many parts, functioned seamlessly. Welch is not above criticism, though. His style and business approach continues to be hotly debated and judged. That said, the numbers don't lie.

For whatever has been said about Welch, his focus on the system as a whole was unparalleled by other CEOs. His strategy, the overall organizational structure of the company, and the management systems revolutionized how General Electric operated. He maintained a persistent and unapologetic approach to improve the company by understanding the interconnectedness of different parts of the company and how they functioned together. He capitalized on the very best ideas from those closest to the work, and empowered people by removing bureaucracy and policies that may have looked good but did not produce results.

One way that he achieved this was by creating a "boundaryless organization" that capitalized on the diversity and unique minds of those in the company, regardless of their department (Ashkenas, 2015). He quit relying on traditional business metrics and was obsessed with performance results. Welch employed "work-outs"—problem-solving processes that created collaboration and dialogue among those doing the work and those leading the company.

Although breaking down silos is nothing new today, it was revolutionary in the 1980s, and Welch aggressively sought to achieve it knowing that it was important to hear from those who were actually performing the tasks that management set forth (Harris, n.d.). His delayering of the organization increased the speed at which decisions could be made and improved an awareness of the problems, their interconnectedness, and how they could be solved.

Despite the controversy surrounding his style, Welch proved the importance of systems thinking, creating multiple avenues of communication, and understanding how each part of the organization functions to support the whole. His process for zooming into a very particular issue while at the same time seeing the organization from 60,000 feet is still studied in business programs today. We believe that you'll see how Welch attacked problems at GE in the new mindshift that we call for in this chapter.

Flawed Thinking: The Absence of Systems Thinking

Understanding the depth and breadth of a problem and all its tentacles is critical for long-term successful problem-solving. We know as leaders that this is an essential professional skill, yet it is not explicitly taught, informally or formally, to the degree that will lead to necessary skill development. Rather, we hope that on-the-job experience will result in better leadership decision-making prowess. Arguably, this leaves a person's growth in this area to chance. This isn't to say that job-embedded learning isn't essential for certain skills, but the theoretical approach of systems thinking that is required for problem-solving has to be understood before it can be applied in practice.

Granted, there are many reasons why this lack of focus on systems thinking occurs. A few that we commonly see are a lack of available time or opportunity for professional learning for school leaders, an overreliance on institutes of higher education graduate programs to train staff, and the inadequate ways to accurately measure educational leadership skills. This prevents the systematic development of leaders from being equipped to deal with the challenges of the 21st century educational system and all of its interconnected parts. Leaders should be provided with ongoing learning opportunities that include measures of their ability to manage change, delegate to a team, communicate clearly, maintain a positive environment, manage conflict, and maximize resources, all connected to their ability to problem-solve given the complexities of the system. Without the necessary skills to look at a problem from every angle, the problems persist and our clarity with the actual issues is muddy at best.

Becoming an expert problem-solver begins with one's ability to understand issues clearly, how a decision may impact something else, and how to move the work forward. It requires an eye on the system as a whole. This way of thinking and approaching problems is needed due to how problems manifest in schools. We typically don't fully engage with a problem until it's entangled in everything we do. This happens because many of our educational issues have moving parts that aren't visible until the problem is already established, and simple solutions are no longer viable. In other words, the issues that plague our schools are like icebergs as shown in Figure 4.1. The formation on the surface is just a small aspect of the massive issues that lie beneath it. To see the whole iceberg for what it is requires several skills and abilities, such as forethought, perceptual acuity, curiosity, synthesis, empathy, and collaboration. We can hear Jack Welch asking, "What's the reality?"

Facing reality includes uncovering all of the details of the issue and identifying the unintended consequences of any given solution. The very nature of problems and how each situation touches another in some form is why The Octopus Approach works. It holistically addresses the issues and the solutions that may cause new problems. Being aware of the interconnectedness

4.1 The Iceberg Illusion

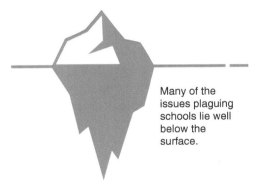

Many of the issues plaguing schools lie well below the surface.

Image source: madartzgraphics/pixabay.com

of programs and functions of a school enables leaders to solve problems with whole system thinking, ensuring that each element is functioning successfully. Because all functions of a school are both independent and connected, they need to be treated that way. They're often not, and that's why problems persist.

Becoming an expert problem-solver begins with one's ability to understand issues clearly, how a decision may impact something else, and how to move the work forward.

Consider a common issue: a high school bus arriving late to school. On the surface, it is a simple management task. A few late passes are distributed, a morning announcement to the staff is made, some extra breakfasts are set aside, and the situation is handled. Undoubtedly, schools manage these situations well, each and every day. But one late bus can create a significant domino effect. It can impact a later bus run for the elementary school, leaving children at the bus stop significantly longer than expected. Or a student who was on the last bus may miss an important quiz or key information presented in class that now he'll have to stay after class to learn. But, he watches his younger sister after school, and if he can't, it creates a serious hardship for his mom. Maybe it prevents an assistant principal from completing an observation because she gets sidetracked with the late bus arrival and getting the students to class as efficiently as possible. How about the teacher who prepared the lesson for the observation and now may need to complete another pre-observation form, have another meeting, and rearrange her plans to make room in the day for both. What seems to be an uneventful problem can have a ripple effect that can have so many unexpected impacts.

These are little inconveniences amid a myriad of hundreds more issues on any given school day. But, framing the situation as simply a late bus misses the relationship and interconnectedness within schools and the need for clear, aligned, systems. It's not a matter of just dealing with the issue. Effective leaders must be keenly aware of the implications that even the smallest disruptions have on teaching and learning. Extrapolate this to a much bigger and more systemic problem, and you have a crisis.

Schools are made up of many parts that all serve specific and necessary functions, and if one part is misaligned, the entire organization will suffer. Issues like teacher morale, student tardiness, family engagement, and more are all things that we live with and often discuss, maybe even mobilize an effort to help solve. But mostly these efforts are short-lived and are tangential to our real problems. They are often symptoms of something greater. The charge for the school leader is to identify the parts of the issue that aren't functioning properly, understand the context of the misalignment, and pursue a solution that will be sustainable. Unfortunately, this isn't what we find in many schools. Issues are dealt with singularly versus approaching them with a systems view.

For organizations to find solutions that work, there "must be a deep understanding of the system or systems they are trying to change and all the factors that shape it" (Kirsch, Bildner, & Walker, 2016). In other words, leaders need a deep and thorough understanding of the systems in order to implement solutions that will provide meaningful and better outcomes.

One thing that we want to explicitly point out is that problems in education may be caused by the system itself. The school system, along with all its inherent facets, policies, and ingrained practices, comprises an industrial standard for how it works to educate, or not, the students we serve. This is also why the system perpetuates itself. Its design is flawed, and outsiders—including policy makers and critics of schooling—can't and won't fix it. It will take insiders, educators with boots on the ground, to think differently and restructure the system. This is the power in the "boundaryless organization." No one person can know it all and those in the trenches need to be at the heart of the problems if we want to solve them.

A FOREVER CHANGING LANDSCAPE

One main problem that educators face is the forever changing landscape in what it means to be a successful school. Consider what US public schools experienced when the federal accountability system changed. When the Every Student Succeeds Act (ESSA) replaced No Child Left Behind (NCLB), not only did the specific metrics change to determine if a school was meeting standards, but ESSA brought back a focus on Trauma Informed Practices, Social Emotional Learning, and Career and Technical Education measures. These efforts aren't new, but since NCLB took a hard line on standardized tests, quantitative data, and school turnaround efforts, many schools adopted programs and efforts to simply improve test scores or face serious consequences. These efforts are a perfect example of working to solve a problem—test scores—without addressing all of the other interconnected aspects of how the problem came to be in the first place.

Any effort that doesn't take into account the whole child, which is very difficult to quantify, is shortsighted and unsustainable. Schools in the 21st century work with students far beyond the 3Rs (reading, writing, and arithmetic). That said, there must be a balance between the social and emotional needs of our students and their academic success. The balance is provided in knowing that both are important as individual characteristics of achievement in school but that they're also one in the same.

To work toward this parity, there are four critical mistakes that leaders must avoid:

TIPS FOR AVOIDING COMMON MISTAKES

1. Understand the core of the problem before implementing a solution.

2. Treat the cause of the problem, rather than the solution.

3. Be flexible. Do not mandate wholesale general solutions for unique situations.

4. Do not make rash, compliance-based decisions.

The answer for leaders who want to avert these four mistakes when working to solve problems is systems thinking. But naming systems thinking as the answer is futile if leaders don't make the mindshift or have specific tools to immerse themselves in fresh efforts toward old problems.

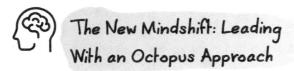

The New Mindshift: Leading With an Octopus Approach

There are multiple places in education where Leading with an Octopus Approach would be instrumental. Among these opportunities are Diversity, Equity, and Inclusion efforts, multitiered systems of support, and grading practices. The complexities of these problems require a systems approach to ensure that all aspects of a solution are addressed. As you read through the chapter, areas in your school will likely come to mind where leading with an Octopus Approach would be helpful.

Composed of eight arms, nine brains, and three hearts, an octopus is a fascinating creature—highly adaptable to their environments, flexible, and advanced (National Wildlife Federation and Oceana, n.d.). The eight arms are controlled by their own brains which are connected to the ninth main brain in the body. Essentially, the primary brain sends messages to the eight, who then act independently to achieve an objective. With three hearts, an octopus uses "one for circulating blood throughout the body and two to pass blood over the gills to oxygenate it" (Flory, 2007).

"Octopuses are renowned for their smarts. . .and most of their 130 million IQ-raising neurons are located not in their brains but along their eight tentacles" (Nuwer, 2013). Researchers believe that octopuses are the grand champions of multitasking because each arm, using its own thought process, can work independently as well as within a system of thinking and processing all at the same time.

The eight arms of an octopus can be a great analogy for the inner workings of a school. All eight arms can work independently and in isolation of each other except that there's a central brain that functions to connect their efforts to achieve a goal, which can be as complicated as camouflaging the skin to seek refuge from prey or pushing through the water as a single unit. The problem with simply applying this analogy to schools is that while schools certainly have multiple arms that work to reach very independent goals, they often don't have a central "brain" that unifies the arms to tackle a problem. What schools need is to behave more like an octopus, allowing the "arms" to use their "brains" independently as well as bringing them together with an awareness of how each function so that we operate as a system.

This is what we call *Leading With an Octopus Approach, a* mindshift *that incorporates systems thinking as a way to solve problems.* We would like to believe that systems thinking was more common in schools, but as we said in the previous section, it demands training and that's not currently the case for enough school leaders. We break down systems thinking by using a model called L.I.S.T. so that you gain an understanding of how The Octopus Approach to change works in schools as long as you're attentive to all four parts of the model.

MODEL: LEARNING, INDEPENDENT PARTS, SENSEMAKING, AND TEMPERAMENT (L.I.S.T.)

Systems thinking is defined several ways, but at its core it is about recognizing the complex parts of a whole so that there is a clear understanding of how each part is interrelated. The idea is applied to problem-solving so that the larger context of any problem is at the forefront of the thinking before applying a new theory of action. Systems thinking is a powerful way that leaders can create a unified perspective before moving into action by accounting for everyone's unique perspective. Ultimately, systems thinking is about being focused on the bigger picture. Failing to do this compounds issues because the dynamics and complexities are misunderstood, and solutions are then misaligned. If the octopuses' brains were not communicating with one another well, the arms may operate independent of one another but never together. That actually may be okay most of the time, but not when the stakes are high. One of the most crucial times when the octopus unifies the brains to the central hub is when prey are near. The same is true for schools and systems thinking; the bigger and more persistent the problem, the greater the need for a systems approach.

L.I.S.T. (shown in Figure 4.2) is an organizational tool, which is at the core of systems thinking because it is designed to produce and uncover, through listing, all the necessary parts of the systems that are intertwined with one another. Organizations that excel at systems thinking are *learning* oriented, recognizing the *interdependent parts* of the whole, while understanding the context of the system through *sensemaking* and the employment of the right *temperament* to build the relationships necessary for sustainable change.

The L.I.S.T. adds structure to The Octopus Approach by combining all of the technical aspects of interdependency and sensemaking that are bookended by the soft skills of learning and temperament. Let's dive deeper into each part of the model so that you can use the Octopus Approach on your school's problems.

4.2 Model: Learning, Interdependent Parts, Sensemaking, and Temperament

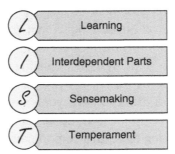

Learning

> We define learning within systems thinking as the discipline of self-improvement and organizational development.

The more a leader learns, the more they develop their capacity, the greater they equip themselves with the skills to handle complex situations. As Nelson and Stolterman (2003) describe in *The Design Way*, "in our struggle to understand an ever more complex reality, we believe the current traditions of inquiry and action prevalent in our society do not give us the support we need—as leaders and designers—to meet the emergent challenges that now confront us." As you'll learn in Chapter 6, inquiry and action alone, without a model for decision-making, lead to very limited solutions and rarely consider the complexities of an issue.

A key characteristic of a systems thinker is that they're a learner. School leaders must continually develop and grow, to evolve and adapt in order to manage the ever-changing world of a school.

Interdependent Parts

> We define interdependent parts within systems thinking as understanding how each part functions, the purpose they serve, and how they contribute to the whole system.

One requirement of systems thinking is that all of the moving parts are known, identified, and empowered. Consider the octopus: on the arms of the octopus there are hundreds of suction cups all working to grip, pull, smell, taste "...individually controlled [so that] they can be isolated to rotate, grasp, and feel the surface as they deem best to meet the goal" (American Oceans, n.d.).

Knowing the parts is just the start. By understanding how they function, which purpose they serve, and how they contribute to the whole system is essential. Each part plays a specific role and has a relationship with other parts. In other words, each part functions individually *and* as a fraction of the whole. Recognizing this is especially important so that when leaders make decisions in one area, they and their team recognize and know how it will initiate a domino effect in other areas.

In addition to understanding that there are independent parts, every leader must develop the ability to "use both a telescope and a microscope," as Jon Gordon has been known to say (Jones & Vari, 2017). Systems thinkers often refer to this as zooming in and zooming out to gain the appropriate perspective at any given time. This degree of focus enables the leader to develop this critical skill of zooming to view issues from multiple angles and spaces—from a grand scale to a minute detail. This allows the leader to see how each arm of the school's operations works alone but also together. This is how leaders begin to make sense of a problem and how entwined our biggest problems are within the system.

Sensemaking

> We define sensemaking within systems thinking as the ability to know the context, understand the system, and bring clarity to an issue.

Every school organization has several arms composed of smaller supporting entities. Think of a first-grade elementary team as an arm. Let's use Figure 4.3 on the next page as an example of the need to know context before problem-solving.

All of this means that there are hundreds of moving parts, and each has its own context. Karl Weick, organizational psychologist, coined the term "sensemaking" as the leadership skill in

4.3 Elements Within a First-Grade Classroom

First-Grade Classroom	
Personnel	• First-Grade Team Lead Teacher • Teachers • Paraprofessionals • Classroom Aids
Students	• Cognitive Ability/Learning Disabilities • Students with Interrupted Formal Education (SIFE) • English Language Learners • Socio-Economic Status
Facilities	• Classroom Space • Resources • Furniture • Desks
Technology	• Assistive Technology Devices • Interactive Technology Devices

understanding the context of situations to draw out issues needing a solution. "Executives who are strong in this capability know how to quickly capture the complexities of their environment and explain them to others in simple terms" (Ancona, Malone, Orlikowski, & Senge, 2007). For systems thinking to be at its best, teams have to engage in sense-making as a precursor to problem-solving. Understanding the true nature or an issue is the only way for a solution to be complete.

In our first-grade classroom example, systems thinkers won't just change personnel without understanding the other context involved with the scenario. This is clearly a classroom with varying degrees of student needs—from learning disabilities to language deficits. The first-grade team leader is currently the teacher. If she retires, a brand-new teacher would be hard pressed to take over and do well, yet we see it all the time in schools. Without context, the function of hiring is absent of the necessary qualities that the position demands.

We define temperament within systems thinking as our ability to stay calm, show care, and build relationships between people and departments.

Temperament is vital in every scenario, but it's even more critical when embracing the crisis mindset. Maintaining the correct temperament keeps leaders in the right frame of mind to not only think clearly but also to hear clearly—to listen and engage productively with team members.

Complex issues are dynamic, and traditional problem-solving methods fall short. Instead, leaders must bring calm to a scenario, show care for the team of people interested in identifying the moving parts and making sense of them for a solution, and build the relationships necessary between people and departments for viable solutions to be created. Baldoni, executive coach and author, says that "temperament is a strong attribute of leadership; those with a temperament that is more focused on others will be those who can lead the most effectively." Systems thinkers have to be focused on the calm that's needed to bring people together to solve problems that will otherwise persist for years to come. They listen as they learn how to build bridges between people and departments within the school.

L.I.S.T. is the practical model for understanding and processing information using systems thinking. It allows leaders to use the Octopus Approach to solve problems. The traditional linear and deductive style problem-solving in schools won't work for perennial issues because persistent problems are always entangled within multiple interconnected aspects of the system. Inquiry and action style problem-solving are like using brute force against something that is impossible to move.

Systems thinking is a far more nuanced approach to understanding problems at their deepest level. It requires a learner's approach, an understanding of the connection regarding the interdependent parts, the ability to make sense of the context, and the temperament to slow down and demonstrate care. Remember that although an octopus is 90 percent muscle, it is also agile and adaptable enough to fit into very small spaces and camouflage itself at a moment's notice. One last point about the Octopus Approach, with three hearts, we believe it has the ability to care more than other species, similar to the leaders who chose to read this book because they want to tackle education's biggest problems.

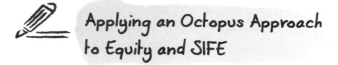

Applying an Octopus Approach to Equity and SIFE

A terrific example of where the Octopus Approach is needed is within the pursuit of equity within all of our schools. This work needs to occur at a systemic level to be effective. The idea and pursuit of equity in our schools is not new but in the last couple of years it has grown dynamically with schools looking at learning outcomes and the environments students are learning in. From engaging students in curriculum talks to helping them amplify their voice as self-advocates. To review practices and policies and ensure resources are supportive and not only punitive.

As communities change in so many ways, we look to see how our schools can be nimble and adjust to meet the many needs of our students, particularly students with interrupted formal education (SIFE). Educating English Language Learners in our schools is not new, but SIFE students who are two or three grade levels below in their native language are attending schools across the United States and to provide them with a meaningful and equitable education will require a new level of thinking.

MAKING THE CONNECTION: EQUITY IN SCHOOLS AND SIFE

Equity in schools is a guarantee that there are no differences in the quality of the educational experience from student to student, school to school, district to district, or state to state. Every *single* student has an opportunity. Every *single* student has access. Recognizing the interconnectedness and impact of equity within every facet of the school system is better actualized through the Octopus Approach. This effort begins with an understanding of what equity is and how it functions within the school from a systems standpoint. Cobb and Krownapple say it this way: "In order to achieve equity, enormous and fundamental changes are necessary, and many of us who are well-served by the current system are reluctant to upset the status quo" (2019, p. 180). If that's not the making of a crisis, then what is?

It is also critical to distinguish equity from equality. Both are extremely important, committed to serving and representing marginalized students, but they are also very different. Although equality and equity are often used interchangeably, there are essential distinctions. Equity is the ongoing pursuit within our schools to make sure that every student is honored as an individual and has the necessary resources regarding their personal learning needs. While equality hinges on access to programs and opportunities, equity brings to account whether or not access leads to enrollment and success. "Said differently, equity becomes the vehicle to equality, but equality can never be the strategy. Equality is the goal. Equity is the strategy" (Kafele, 2021).

When leaders strive to ensure a culture of equity in their schools, several challenges inevitably arise. One of the first questions that should be asked is what are the barriers to equity, especially after nearly a lifetime has passed since the *Brown v. Board of Education* decision in 1954 (US Government Accountability Office, 2016). This slower than snail's pace progress is why understanding the intricacies of the school system, revealing might be festering inequity, through an

Octopus Approach is a vital first step. As we look to ensure that each student has the same opportunity and access as every other student, analyzing enrollment within all programs— offering rigorous curriculum, developing a community of learners, and providing students the support they need—we need to understand how being more equitable fits into the greater system of the school. If the whole system is not considered, we run the risk of our equity focus being eclipsed by policies and procedures that are systemic in nature, and can be insensitive to the unique needs of marginalized populations (NHSS, 2021).

As an aside, this is the power of Jack Welch's management strategies described earlier, such as the "boundaryless organization" and delayering of hierarchical structures that impede progress by complicating the system and creating bureaucracy. Providing equitable classrooms is a perennial problem that educational leaders continually work to solve but without being able to clearly hear and learn from those closest to the work, efforts will fall short.

Although a relatively small population of students, Students with Interrupted Formal Education (SIFE) students require an intensive approach to education. Due to their circumstances and needs, they represent the extent to which schools must go in order to create equitable schooling. SIFE are defined as:

> English Language Learners (ELLs) who have attended schools in the United States for less than twelve months and who, upon initial enrollment in such schools, are two or more years below grade level in literacy in their home language and/or two or more years below grade level in Math due to inconsistent or interrupted schooling prior to arrival in the United States. (NYSED, n.d.)

SIFE offer a complexity to equitable schooling as a perennial problem in education due to the magnitude of challenges they present, and the resources needed which may not be readily available in all schools. Many of the issues that educators are trying to solve for other groups—below grade level literacy and numeracy, social and emotional trauma, displacement, and a myriad of other challenges—are also prevalent for SIFE. In fact, one single child may suffer from *all* of the challenges that schools are trying to solve.

Let's use the Octopus Approach for equity, including SIFE as one of the arms. Because an equitable education is a perennial problem, we need a new way to think about it if we want to begin to make changes. The impact of each decision must be weighed so one group doesn't benefit while another is over-looked. This means that every group of students who don't meet the educational outcomes intended for all kids needs to be cared for in different but systemic ways. What may be good for one group of students in terms of equity may not be equitable for another. Blanket strategies for making education equitable don't consider the complexities of each group of students or each student individually for that matter.

For this reason, we turn to L.I.S.T. First, we must *learn* everything we can about each group of students in our schools. Leaders who commit to learning everything they can about students, their communities, and the issues they face are more equipped to see the problems for what they are. They zoom in and zoom out to see the intricacies as well as the big picture. Second, and maybe the most important aspect of the Octopus Approach, we must understand SIFE as one arm of our equity problem and its individual as well as *interconnected* nature to provide a more equitable experience for all stu-dents. We can't tackle equity until we look at each area of inequity as both unique but also linked to one another.

Third, so much of what occurs in the life of SIFE is misunder-stood. Leaders must spend time *sensemaking*, looking into the context and building relationships with families and the ser-vices they require. And, finally, when we approach these scenarios with the right *temperament* as leaders we're far more likely to become accepted into the communities we seek to serve. For many schools, the leadership team is practically a foreigner to the groups of students and their families who experience the greatest educational inequities. Focusing on temperament is critical in terms of showing care and building partnerships.

The Octopus Approach teaches leaders to think about each aspect of the school as its own function yet connected to the larger system as a whole.

The opportunity to tackle equity in schools lies within our ability to use systems thinking to work *for* all rather than against them. SIFE is just one example of the equity needs of students in our schools. They represent a very small portion of our student population, but also demand intensive attention and necessary resources that will challenge even the best systems. They are very unique but also interconnected with all other efforts for a more equitable outcome for all students. The Octopus Approach teaches leaders to think about each aspect of the school as its own function yet connected to the larger system as a whole.

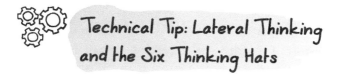

Technical Tip: Lateral Thinking and the Six Thinking Hats

To solve issues such as the ones associated with SIFE and the equitable outcomes for all students, we need a level of candor that Jack Welch possessed. Candor is not a personality trait, it's a skill. Therefore, we need a tool to help us think differently and more creatively.

In education, we often associate creativity with the arts, and for good reason, but it doesn't end there. Original thinking, new ideas, and patterns can emerge on the tapestry of problem-solving with the right approach. In fact, they must.

Abandoning traditional methods of resolving crises is how Jerry Sternin was able to successfully curb malnourishment in southern rural Vietnam. Sternin sought out the bright spots in the rural communities, villages where malnourishment wasn't afflicting the community, yet lived in the same harsh conditions as ones where malnourishment was a problem. His methodology, inquisitive pursuit, and unrelenting will created an openness to ideas that yielded results. He approached the problem as a learner, with that Beginner's Mind, he looked for interconnectivity, he tried to make sense of the issue, and he slowed down to build relationships among the people. He solved an unsolvable problem (Sternin & Choo, 2000).

Although schools are very complex organisms, and the perennial problems may seem insurmountable, the Octopus Approach provides the framework to codify and understand the organization's various elements; we use L.I.S.T. to accomplish this. Lastly, we want to use a proven formula to think critically. Having a canvas, possessing the right tools and mediums, is only the preparatory aspect of the artist's pursuit. At some point, she must paint. Edward De Bono's Six Thinking Hats is a great way to creatively "rumble" (Brown, 2019) with persistent problems using systems' thinking even when the canvas of the problem seems to be staring back with nothing to say.

As shown in Figure 4.4, each hat plays a very specific role to help frame, analyze, discuss, and solve issues. This powerful tool not only guarantees that various aspects of the issue will be laid out, discussed and vetted, it also reduces the hierarchy and fear that is often present on teams who have a problem to solve. Consider the Black Hat. The individual who wears this hat is responsible for being critical and sending up red flags. The person is empowered to do so, and a good leader, who knows the team well, will align the individual's strengths to the various hats.

The hats allow for titles and positions to take a back seat to the responsibility of the person wearing the hat. Candor is a

4.4 Six Thinking Hats (De Bono, 2016)

Thinking Hat		Purpose	Role
Blue	The Conductor's Hat	Thinking about and managing the thinking process	The Blue Hat is the control hat. It is used for metacognition. It sets the agenda, including focus and sequence, ensures the guidelines are observed and asks for summaries, conclusions, decisions, and plans for action.
Green	The Creative Hat	Generating ideas	The Green Hat is for generating new ideas, alternatives, possibilities, and new concepts.
Red	For the Heart	Intuition and feelings	The Red Hat invites feelings without justification. It considers intuition and instincts.
Yellow	The Optimist's Hat	Benefits and values	The Yellow Hat is for a positive view of things. It looks for the upside of situations.

(Continued)

4.4 (Continued)

Thinking Hat		Purpose	Role
Black	The Judge's Hat	Caution	The Black Hat identifies risk. It is used for critical judgment and must give the logical reasons for concerns. It is one of the most powerful hats.
White	The Factual Hat	Information	The White Hat is all about facts and data. What information is known, what is needed, and where can it be found?

Image source: DenEmmanuel/istock.com

prerequisite to successfully discussing issues and the hats empower individuals with a voice. It is essential to acknowledge that each role of the hat is important. If the Black Hat begins to challenge ideas and successfully reveals problems that could thwart any real action, then the White Hat is responsible for not letting the conversation stop there, which usually happens. Conversational dead ends shouldn't exist. Rather, the White Hat should jump in to pursue additional facts and information.

This degree of communication and level of dialogue is what is needed to successfully explore all elements of a situation. The last thing we want to do is overlook issues or fail to explore ideas that could solve long-term problems. The Six Thinking

Hats is a tool for leaders who are learning to be more systems-minded. It works with The Octopus Approach because it forces us to think about all the moving parts and how each is connected.

Reflection Questions

1. What would a boundaryless school look like?

2. What issues does your school face that require systems thinking?

3. Consider one of your perennial problems. What would an Octopus Approach reveal about the arms of the problem?

4. Consider one of your perennial problems. How might a L.I.S.T. approach help you tackle the problem?

MINDSHIFT #5: LEADING WITH A DISCIPLINED TUNNEL VISION

I know of no case study in history that describes an organization that has been managed out of a crisis. Every single one of them was led.

—Simon Sinek (2014)

In Ed Catmull's *Creativity Inc.*, he describes what Pixar calls their Braintrust. At its core, the Braintrust is a process for movie creators to get feedback so that they can improve their films. It brings together a group of people to watch a movie at critical times during its creation. Behavior during a Braintrust session is clearly guided by core values, including the use of candor about what needs to be improved for the movie to be better, more cohesive, and clearer for the viewer.

The Braintrust was established because directors get tunnel vision. Catmull says that "people who take on complicated creative projects become lost at some point in the process ... where once he or she could see a forest, now there are only trees ... in order to create, you must internalize and almost become the project for a while, and that near-fusing with the project is an essential part of its emergence" (p. 91). The paradox is that the tunnel vision necessary to make the film succeed can also hinder the director's ability to see flaws during parts of its creation. The tunnel vision needed for the directors to immerse themselves in the project must then be balanced through discipline. The Braintrust helps with that need.

Braintrust participants are trained, through experiencing Braintrust sessions and the established culture of candor that they bring, to notice parts of the film that don't work well or that aren't fully developed. Catmull describes the nuances that the Braintrust might uncover that others may miss, even whether or not the rules in the make-believe world of the film are consistent with one another. Have you ever noticed in the movie *Ratatouille* that all the rats walk on all four paws except for Remy "whose upright posture sets him apart" as the main character (p. 97)? The Braintrust dissects the film in ways that the writers and directors can't because their heads are down, doing the work. As the writers and directors sustain their tunnel vision, the Braintrust provides the discipline to otherwise view the important details of making a film with greater accuracy, precision, and focus.

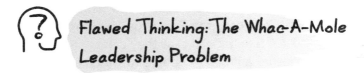

Flawed Thinking: The Whac-A-Mole Leadership Problem

Medical News Today warns readers that if they experience tunnel vision, otherwise known as peripheral vision loss, they "should seek medical help as soon as possible to help prevent permanent vision loss." When a person's peripheral vision isn't working well, it's a sign that they eventually won't be able to see at all. We believe that prolonged tunnel vision by educational leaders has resulted in institutional inattentiveness to the root causes of the crises affecting schools.

It's why we end up unable to detect the underlying reasons for the issues that deserve our full attention. There are a myriad of causes for losing hold of goals and nothing should excuse us from dealing with our chronic problems, but identifying some of the ways in which we end up focused on the wrong issues can help us understand how to set a target on our real crises. A common hindrance is confusing busyness with effectiveness. Anyone can fill a schedule with to-dos, appointments, and urgent work to tackle. But leaders who operate this way are not only ineffective, they're also likely unfulfilled. Full days do not result in fulfilled duties, and a lack of results leads to discouragement.

> The mere fact that we're "getting the work done" does not mean that the school or district is making progress.

Moreover, efficiency is not the same as effectiveness. The two are often confused. Even our most efficient leaders—those who schedule and finish tasks ahead of time, complete processes to maintain compliance, and consistently attend meetings based on a calendar of activities—are not necessarily the most effective. The mere fact that we're "getting the work done" does not mean that the school or district is making progress. Busyness and low-level activities lure us into believing that when our heads are down and we're working hard that we're accomplishing meaningful quality work. That's not always true.

Worse yet, "when we're busy and stressed, we often default to working on whatever has the most imminent deadline, even if it's not particularly important" (Boyes, 2018). The more that we feel the weight of the job, the more that we narrow our scope of the work that needs to be done. An inability to step back and see the whole picture means that our main priorities go unmet. The undertaking of running a school, by itself, even without attending to the learning needs of the students or focusing on teaching practices, is daunting. We tell ourselves that we'll get to the bigger and more important issues in the near future, as soon as we deal with the current scenario, but that future never comes. We end up suffering from the negative impact of our tunnel vision.

"Managers sometimes think and operate linearly—one thing at a time—or get so involved in a project or problem that they neglect to see what is going on around them" (Decker & Mitchell, 2016). We contend that education's crises are perpetuated by the flawed thinking that comes with tunnel vision in that we end up feeling like we need to attend to the problems of the day versus the ones that have lasted the tests of time. We call this the Whac-A-Mole Leadership Problem.

WHAC-A-MOLE LEADERSHIP

Managing the day through tunnel vision is exhausting. In fact, it's scary. The unpredictability and elusiveness create a sense of urgency whereby every facet of daily school leadership becomes a crisis, and our real crises vanish into the oblivion of the day, week, and year. Anyone who has played the carnival game Whac-A-Mole knows what it feels like to be head-down waiting for the next mole to emerge. The moles are silly— laughing, jumping, and jeering the contestant. If you've played the game against others at a carnival, you know that you have to hit a number of moles in a finite time to be the winner. If you've played the version as a video game, the moles come faster and faster until the time runs out. It's unlikely that you'll hit them all, and you can't see anyone or anything around you except the moles directly in front of you. You hear the noise, the commotion, but you miss the totality of the event.

In a *New York Times* article about financial management, Ron Lieber (2016) made the case that understanding how to invest well is similar to the Whac-A-Mole game. "The seeming pace of change, of action, makes it feel as if we need to react at twitch speed, too." Lieber goes on to say that "hair-trigger decision making on investing or spending quite often leads to regret." This is precisely the feeling we get when we're under the allure and beguile of tunnel vision. On one end, tunnel vision can feel out of control. On the other hand, this Whac-A-Mole leadership style can be "action-packed," addicting, and satisfying when we get to the end of the day, believing that we survived, again. We won.

There's an addictive attraction when leading with tunnel vision that seduces us into believing that we're effective as long as the place doesn't burn to the ground. We somehow believe that you can't hit all of the moles, but if you "whac" more than the school next door, you're better off. It might feel good to lead this way given the frenetic pace of schools, but it won't solve the deeper problems that continue to haunt student achievement. But maybe we can use the obsessive game-like habits of tunnel vision to attack perennial problems, by seeking a tunnel vision instead of avoiding one.

THE TUNNEL VISION PARADOX

There's a paradox in what happens when we get tunnel vision; while on the one hand tunnel vision prevents us from focusing on the big picture, on the other hand, it can also help us to focus on a problem when we use it to our advantage. What this tells us is that leaders can harness the benefits of this mindshift for valuable use. If we can *get* tunnel vision, we can *use* tunnel vision.

The fact is that poorly executed tunnel vision stems from a lack of focus on the purpose and vision of the school. Its origin is likely from a lack of accountability anchored to a set of pre-determined goals. And without identified time-bound goals, we are unable to refocus ourselves when we become distracted. This is especially true in an environment where there are so many fires to put out. Ironically, we end up with the gratification of feeling like problem-solvers, but we only ever manage the immediate crises and not the perennial problems.

The mindshift necessary to move from the reactive Whac-A-Mole Leadership Problem to a proactive leadership style requires focus and discipline. We call this new mindshift a Disciplined Tunnel Vision (DTV).

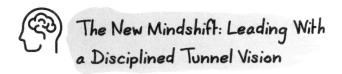

The New Mindshift: Leading With a Disciplined Tunnel Vision

Disciplined Tunnel Vision is defined by *an unwavering determination to change the status quo through a process that leads to a difference in the beliefs, behaviors, and outcomes for the people within the organization.* DTV reverses the norm by altering current conditions. When leaders use this mindshift, they are able to encourage others, including the students, the staff, and the community, to believe and behave in new ways that ultimately reach desired results for school and district success.

The transformation in the switch toward a DTV starts with setting a vision that provides complete clarity on what needs to be achieved. This work should remind leaders about the strategic nature of a strong school culture. Included in the drivers of every successful culture are a sense of purpose, trust, accountability, support, growth, and innovation at the center of the work (Jones, Thomas-EL, & Vari, 2020). We leaders follow our model for DTV, and they accomplish that.

You should find some familiarity in the following model. Many schools have done some level of vision and mission work. What schools miss are the steps thereafter in maintaining the focus necessary to bring about true changes that result in better outcomes for students. Note as you move through the model that it's a practical set of steps that can be followed for any initiative to be successful.

MODEL: VISION, VALUES, KPIS, PRINCIPLES, FOCUS, AND MODELS

We argue that the recurring problems in schools are not foreign to school and district leaders. They are well known and documented in much of the research about what needs to change in education. But that doesn't mean that we have the tools necessary to make any significant changes any time soon. Change is a messy work. We won't argue that. But what we often find is that although school leadership is complex, it doesn't have to be complicated. Any leader can follow steps toward a change, and that's what we're proposing is the discipline necessary to see the change we seek to make in action.

What we often find is that although school leadership is complex, it doesn't have to be complicated.

Kotter (1996) authored an eight-step process for managing change, and we know of varying schools of educational leadership that use his *Leading Change* book in study. In practice, though, change initiatives aren't driven by theory. In fact, we contend that much of the educational theory is not put into practice. One of the greatest examples, used in Chapter 2, is all of the research on grading that gets ignored, adorning bookshelves in offices.

Reeves points out that there are several "factors required for change." The first is a conscious "decision to reject the past" and the second is the development of psychological safety in admitting that we have been wrong thus far (2021, p. 16). Thus, a prerequisite for vision-setting is letting go of what we've done to this point because it hasn't gotten us the results we want for all of our students.

What is helpful to educational leaders is a template—a model to follow and build within the culture. Note that many of the mindshifts in this book work in tandem. Isolating them limits their effectiveness. Coupling two together increases the power of each and their aptitude for producing your desired results. For example, the vision, values, and goals section in this chapter should be executed with a team which has already completed the important, urgent, and persistent crisis filter from Chapter 1. Leadership is always directional, and we want to be sure that we're leading in the right direction.

The model in Figure 5.1 is not intended to support the vision that you have now, but rather to support a recalibrated vision that is aligned to a different mentality about leading change in your school. The difference with this new model is the discipline and collaboration it requires in carrying out all six steps. We call it our Six-Step Practical Change Model because the steps are meant to be carried out with teams *in practice*, and each step is meant to be executed within the school environment. By applying this model in action, school leaders are leading with a DTV that will produce real change.

Step #1: Set the Vision and Mission

We know from our work in schools that the first few steps in the six steps to a DTV will be familiar, but we want to give our

5.1 Model: Vision, Values, KPIs, Principles, Focus, and Models

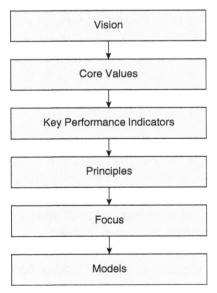

school partners a new way to think about vision and mission work. The first difference in this model, versus any other, is that we don't require you to develop a mission for the school; this isn't to suggest that mission statements are superfluous. We bring them to life at the department, committee, task force, and initiative levels. In other words, this model begins by establishing a vision statement for the school and mission statements for departments and other groups within the school community.

As we've done vision work with schools around the country, a commonality that we see is that vision statements are often convoluted. These statements are filled with "edujargon" and tend to read like long, boring, ambiguous, utopic nonsense by attempting to address everyone and everything about school and the world. The more succinct, specific, and unique the statement, the better.

It should also be direct, memorable, definitive, and tailored to the school. Creating a vision statement isn't a box to be checked or an ideological approach to our philosophy about schooling. Instead, the statement should be practical enough to answer three specific questions for the school and community: what do we desire to accomplish; who do we want the work to benefit; and why does it matter?

> The vision of ABC Elementary School is to equip young people with the skills and mindsets to be and feel effective as lifelong learners.

Next, based on the school's vision statement, each division of the school should develop their own mission statement to uniquely support the vision—the math department, the PTA/PTO, the grading committee, the fifth-grade team, and the reading curriculum task force. Every division of the school should have a mission statement, and they all start the same way: "The mission of the (insert school division) is to uphold the vision of our school by..." and the rest of the statement includes what the department, committee, or team actually should do in practice. The following is a math department's mission statement that uses the sentence stem:

> The mission of the math department is to uphold the vision of our school by fostering math literacy that builds number sense.

The PTA/PTO also aligns their mission statement to the vision:

> The mission of the PTO is to uphold the vision of our school by hosting family events that promote social and emotional wellness.

The grading committee uses the same format to craft their mission statement:

> The mission of the grading committee is to uphold the vision of our school by including peer feedback as part of a comprehensive assessment system.

While it might seem that number sense, social and emotional wellness, and peer feedback are disconnected initiatives, they are the how-to for the overall vision of equipping young people with the skills and mindset to be and feel effective as learners. Each mission offers its unique angle in bringing the vision to light. And, we can both qualitatively and quantitatively measure students' effectiveness as learners as well as how they feel about themselves as learners.

Additionally, the establishment of statements of this kind at the committee and department level provokes a new kind of accountability regarding what each committee needs to accomplish as a team and the work involved to achieve their mission. It also leads nicely into the next step in our Practical Change Model, which is to develop a set of core values to guide the work that the vision articulates.

Step #2: Determine the Core Values

Core values represent the behaviors associated with bringing the vision into fruition. Having more than five core values becomes unwieldy and dilutes their effectiveness and memorability. This is, again, what we commonly see that can go wrong with vision work—confusing and elaborate vision statements and more core values than are feasible to monitor and track. With your team, determine three to five core values that serve as a reference to plan out daily, weekly, and monthly high-leverage activities. They are also great to revisit for reminders of the importance of the work when the challenges of the day become either daunting or nebulous.

Committees that often work with curriculum and instruction initiatives, like department or grade-level teams, might have similar core values that demonstrate the behaviors that we expect from everyone as contributing members of the committee. If someone deviates from these values, everyone will know it. That's what holds us accountable as a team and as individuals. Here's an example of one committee's core values:

1. Everyone commits to our committee's goals.

2. Everyone teaches the models the way they are written.

3. Everyone engages in data-driven discussion to determine next steps when students achieve or don't achieve in accordance with our principles.

At the point in which we have values, committees use school improvement or strategic plan goals to craft very specific targets known as Key Performance Indicators (KPIs) to determine whether or not we're reaching success. The KPIs have to be more granular than the school improvement goal that they are working to achieve. A word of caution: your schoolwide goals and your KPIs should be distinctly different. The schoolwide goals are determined by a school improvement team and handed off to relevant committees to execute initiatives to achieve them.

These types of goals are often written in a SMART goal format, meaning they are Specific, Measurable, Attainable, Relevant, and Time-bound. For example, "By the end of the academic year, math proficiency for Black students will increase by 10 percent as measured on the State Assessment." The committee's job is to break down these school goals into KPIs, which are used to keep the committee aligned to the work and able to track how initiatives contribute to meeting school improvement goals.

Step #3: Establish the Key Performance Indicators

The SMART goal format includes how success will be measured. But, too often, schools set goals using lagging data, such as end-of-year exams and annual standardized assessment scores that aren't retrievable until the learners have moved on to the next grade. That assessment data are powerful for districts, schools, and departments to review for curriculum alignment to the standards, overall instructional practices, and additional goal setting, but it's not helpful for making adjustments to classroom instruction and practice in real time, which is the role of the committees. That's why they need to establish KPIs that support the school improvement goal and serve as mile markers toward the destination.

KPIs measure incremental progress that can be used to predict how a measure that is far off into the distant future will end up. Unless we define these benchmarks, we have no organized or systemic way to know if we are progressing toward a goal. We are left with "I think, I feel" and unreliable data until the final measurement takes place. Without incremental metrics to track performance, no adjustments can be made to the committee's initiatives to prevent a miss on the final target. If this happens, and it often does, a new batch of students arrives and the problem persists again and again, developing into the perpetual nature of a crisis that we're addressing in this book.

The point about the KPIs is simple, though. To make the mindshift to a truly focused and disciplined school culture, obsessed with student achievement, we must establish checkpoints that can be analyzed weekly and daily, not monthly, or yearly. If you don't have day-to-day and unit-to-unit KPIs, we'll be busy for an entire year, but our hard work will not be productive. It will simply be left to chance.

Step #4: Define the Principles

Up until now, you may be thinking, *Seriously—vision, core values, and goals—that's how we're going to accomplish new thinking to solve old problems?* And you may be right about the strategies, but are you right about these practices actually being in place in schools the way we're describing them here? Note the nuances. The vision statement should answer very specific questions about what we do, who it's for, and why it's important; the core values are limited to five or fewer that speak to behavioral expectations for students and staff; and the KPIs are based on daily and weekly data analysis. Review your plans to expose murky statements, tens of core values, poorly written annual goals, and plans that are nice on paper but unrecognizable in reality.

Let's suppose your vetting revealed that you have all three in place and done well—vision, values, and goals (KPIs)—these next three steps are where the laser-like focus and discipline play out in the daily work. Our Six-Step Practical Change Model brings you closer to a DTV approach to attacking problems. Most change initiatives bypass defining the principles that they'll use to differentiate the new practices from the old ones. The best example of principles in use that we know about is at Bridgewater and Associates, one of the most successful investment firms on Earth. Ray Dalio, the CEO, says this about the need for principles: "I know that having tools and protocols is necessary to help people convert what they want to do into actually doing it" (2017, p. 543). Without principles, the vision will remain on paper with very little coming to fruition in practice.

Principles are research-based methods that have demonstrated effectiveness through evidence and research in the field. As an instructional example, John Hattie, Robert Marzano, and others have published lists of effective instructional practices, including their corresponding effect sizes on learning outcomes. Assembling your list of key instructional practices from the research available would be a set of instructional principles identified for your school. For any change initiative to take hold, these new methods, to be used by everyone, should be listed as success practices to take the place of old norms or conditions.

Let's explore how this plays out in a Math Committee. The Committee has a vision statement, core values, and KPIs, all aligned to improving math proficiency for Black students. But what are we going to do differently to achieve success? We're only halfway through the disciplined effort necessary to activate change. We need principles to guide our everyday work. Because our sample school is working on a math goal, the Committee's Principles can focus on what teachers will do differently, how student outcomes will change, or a combination of both.

To illustrate how the principles align with best practices and information that already exist, we chose to share an example of a math team that simply adopted the mathematical practices as their principles for student engagement (Common Core Standards Initiative, 2010).

1. Make sense of problems and persevere in solving them.
2. Reason abstractly and quantitatively.
3. Construct viable arguments and critique the reasoning of others.
4. Model with mathematics.
5. Use appropriate tools strategically.
6. Attend to precision.
7. Look for and make use of structure.
8. Look for and express regularity in repeated reasoning.

We now have eight principles for math success as determined by the Math Committee. Its members know that the mathematical practices can serve as principles to their work so math scores can improve. Ideally, every student, including Black students who are the focus of the school improvement goal, will exhibit these practices daily. However, it's not realistic to master all of them every day or all at once. Therefore, the team's next step is to narrow the focus even more so that we're certain that every teacher and each pupil is actively working toward reaching the goal.

Step #5: Identify a Focus

Keep in mind, if you try to do too much, you will not achieve anything. This is why agreeing on a primary focus within the principles executes a DTV and allows the committee to develop strategies, collect evidence of implementation, and measure progress along the way. The committee determines and communicates to others the expectations that align to the identified focus. Then, a method for accountability and data collection is developed. How will teachers outside the committee know if they're doing it right? What will be the mathematical look-fors when walkthroughs are conducted? That's where the models come into play in Step 6.

As an example, using the math principles from Step #4, our department might be completely focused for a period of time on "students will look for and make use of structure." We might have even pulled this focus from our assessment data as something that students were missing on their way to becoming proficient in math. The entire department becomes very disciplined in how they plan lessons regarding this focus in particular. The reason that we need the models is because even our math teachers might be asking themselves: what does it look like to execute a lesson plan where students are looking for and making use of structure in the math classroom? The model for implementation supports that.

Step #6: Support Implementation With Models

You can see how this is a very in-depth approach to solving a specific problem. The process is not math-specific, it works for school climate teams, behavior goals, and any perennial problem your school might be facing. It's only this type of DTV that gets results with our crises in education. Without it, the same old structures remain, and the same old results endure, year after year. Remember, we started with the norm that we have to abandon past practices, no matter how hard we worked to institute them.

Models are necessary as the final step in our Practical Change Model because they communicate to everyone *how* we will make a change to our practice. The model demonstrates exactly what the new principle—in particular our focus—looks like in action. And, every time we switch the focus to a new principle, we provide new models for how to put the new focus strategy into action. This degree of support for teachers provides for them with a visual, illustration, or example for how they will create the learning experience for children in their particular classroom.

An example of a model that math teachers would use in their lesson plans and classrooms to achieve the focus strategy of having students *look for and use structures* is listening carefully to the academic vocabulary students use when talking about math structures. The model might be a Number Talk that includes a list of keywords that would signal to the teacher (or an observer) that students, more specifically, Black students who are the center of the math goal, are identifying patterns within the math. If, during a Number Talk, two students justified their answers differently, the model would help teachers to recognize when Black students are looking for and using structures and when they are not. For example, if one student says they knew that 8×6 was 48 because they knew 8×5 is 40 and 8 more is 48, they're using a mathematically sound structure to do mental math. If the other student calculates 8×6 as 48 and justifies it by saying that they know their eight facts, then the second student is using memorization and not a mathematical structure. Of course, either method gets to the right answer, but one shows evidence that students are using the mathematical practice, and it's our use of a the Six-Step Practical Change Model of a DTV that allows us to make a difference, from a vision and mission for change all the way through to the use of models that change beliefs, behaviors, and outcomes.

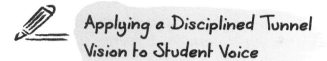

Applying a Disciplined Tunnel Vision to Student Voice

We hope that you can see how this approach can be used to attack all kinds of problems in schools. The discipline is in following all six steps and staying true to each so that people know how to implement the models in practice and that the models are what we believe will improve our student outcomes. To make the connection to education, we provide an example using student voice as the focus for improvement.

Students throughout the country spoke out to call for social justice in America, in what many refer to as the dual pandemics—COVID-19 and Systemic Racism. Particularly, high school age children indicated that they wanted a stronger voice within school discipline policies, curriculum, and instruction, and more. Additionally, when consulting with schools and districts regarding their curriculum, instruction, assessments, feedback cycles, and overall improvements to culture, we find that student voice is either not amplified well and done without a viable strategy or, in some cases, it's discouraged. Not only do students want a voice in the classroom, they deserve it, and it supports their cognitive development and self-efficacy as learners.

MAKING THE CONNECTION: STUDENT VOICE IN THE CLASSROOM

Let's, then, apply DTV and the Six-Step Practical Change Model to a school's improvement goal in elevating student voice in the classroom to support learning. You assemble your Student Voice Team and get to work.

First, we set a mission. *The mission of the Student Voice Team is to uphold the vision of the school by sharing strategies that can support student collaboration for an average of 50 percent of the total instructional time per week.* Next, we determine our core values. *Every classroom is a welcoming space. We value student contributions. Every classroom is a collaborative environment between students and teachers and students and their peers. The person doing the majority of talking is doing the majority of learning.* We know that you can set one or two more. Now it's time for KPIs. You might measure teachers' use of a particular talk protocol to ensure that everyone used it effectively this month. Or you might do classroom visits to measure the percentage of the time that students are talking and collaborating. Maybe your team wants to gather students' perspectives on how they feel their voices are heard.

We move on to defining a set of principles. In this case, we might borrow six to ten collaborative structures from Kagan. But, we're not going to expect everyone to use all ten right away, we're going to narrow the structures down to one or two as the focus for a period of time, maybe even the entire year. Teachers can choose to do any of the principles, but as leaders, we're looking for accurate and precise use of only the one or two that are identified as the focus. To leave no doubt on what the goal for student collaboration looks like, the one or two Kagan structures chosen for the initial focus come with steps as a model for proper implementation, and the instructional team that we put together to lead the work might even record a video of them being done well in a classroom where the teacher's instructions were flawless. This also serves as an excellent way to onboard new teachers down the road, who weren't around during initial implementation but who need to get caught up quickly.

Using DTV, we aren't just saying that we want to amplify student voice, we have a plan down to what it looks like and a measurement that we can use right away. We aren't just handing the staff a list of talk strategies or providing professional development to get better at it, we're strategically focused on the implementation of one or two very specific practices as our focus in Step 5 and the use of the model to implement them from Step 6.

And now that we're all rowing in the same direction, we're finally going to get somewhere. Your team can even double dip if you couple DTV with at least one of the other mindshifts. Imagine using a Battleground Mentality, the Octopus Approach, or a Beginner's Mind while moving through the six steps. Instead of waiting for all of the moles to keep popping up randomly and losing our target, we're treating the true crisis as it should be treated, with a Disciplined Tunnel Vision (Figure 5.2).

5.2 Practical Change Model Applied to Student Voice

6-Step Practical Change Model	Student Voice Team Example
Step #1: Set the Vision and Mission Key: *Use the school vision to develop the team's mission.*	The vision of the Student Voice Team is to uphold the vision of the school by sharing strategies that can support student collaboration for an average of 50 percent of the total instructional time per week.
Step #2: Determine the Core Values Key: *Everyone on the team contributes to the core values; not everyone needs to contribute to the mission.*	1. Every classroom is a welcoming space. 2. We value student contributions. 3. Every classroom is a collaborative environment between students and teachers and students and their peers. 4. The person doing the majority of talking is doing the majority of the learning.
Step #3: Establish the Key Performance Indicators	1. You might measure teachers' use of a

(Continued)

5.2 (Continued)

6-Step Practical Change Model	Student Voice Team Example
Key: The KPIs should be metrics that will help us to reach our goals; they aren't the goals themselves.	particular talk protocol to ensure that everyone used it effectively this month. 2. You might do classroom visits to measure the percentage of the time that students are talking and collaborating. 3. Maybe your team wants to gather students' perspectives on how they feel their voices are heard.
Step #4: Define the Principles *Key: Principles should be research- or evidence-based practices; not a set of beliefs.*	For a set of principles to support student voice, we might adopt Kagan structures for lesson planning and use in the classroom. You might also have an instructional team design 10-12 ways that teachers can get students talking as learners.
Step #5: Identify a Focus *Key: Pick one or two to start; you can't accomplish all of the principles in one month or even one year.*	For the focus, we pick one or two of the principles. In the case of Kagan, we might pick Rally Robin as our one focus strategy for all teachers.
Step #6: Support Implementation with Models *Key: Models communicate exactly what the focus looks like in action; without models, everyone will likely see the change differently from one another.*	We need a model that communicates what Rally Robin looks like in the classroom as it unfolds from lesson planning to student engagement.

Technical Tip: Learning to Notice

Leading with a Crisis Mindset, including a DTV, requires leaders to use a critical eye, especially when visiting the most important spaces in our schools—the classrooms. The greatest impact in student learning comes from the teacher (Lee, 2018), and we know that principals who are instructional leaders have a massive impact on teachers (Bartoletti & Connelly, 2013). Schools that are supportive yet maintain high expectations for staff are not only more likely to see stronger student outcomes but are also more likely to attract and retain top talent (Jones et al., 2020). One of the number one drivers of a successful school, especially in the implementation of best practices and the use of DTV, is feedback. When teachers consistently receive quality feedback in what our friend Aubrey Patterson would call a "warm yet demanding" way, they get better faster.

We have found one major difference between leaders who can provide quality feedback and those whose feedback is mediocre—an intense awareness of all that is going on around them. Leaders who can see what's on the walls, what's being required of students, how much of the time is on task, whether or not the assignments are rigorous, and more within seconds of being in a classroom are able to absorb more and provide higher quality feedback than those who can't do so with speed an expert knowledge of what they see, hear, and feel.

Max Bazerman, Harvard Business School Professor and Codirector of the Harvard Kennedy School's Center for Public Leadership, calls this extreme awareness "the power of noticing." This is our ability to see what others don't and note when we're seeing more than what is actually there. Let's explore this phenomenon further in terms of a DTV.

Whenever we coach leaders to provide quality feedback, we ask six questions about the classroom environment that speak to the essence and art of lesson planning. What is the teacher doing? What are the students doing? What is the task? Is the task aligned to standards? Is the task rigorous? Is technology being used to enhance the lesson? In conducting classroom visits, we find, more often than not, that leaders see an aspect of the lesson that isn't really there. Two examples emerge:

Example #1: What are the students doing? We ask this to a small group of instructional leaders as we debrief a classroom visit. Almost without fail, we hear things like "they were listening" or "they were reading." Neither one of these are things that we can actually measure but we make assumptions about the level of engagement. By asking the question several more times, we may find that students weren't doing much of anything at all. Perhaps the teacher was talking and the students were not. They may have been listening. But, without an authentic activity associated with the learning task, we simply don't know.

Example #2: What was the teacher doing? The respondents often name the strategy that the teacher was supposedly using, for example, "think-pair-share" (TPS). Imagine that the teacher named the strategy—TPS—on her agenda, but then, during execution, the activity only captures the shared aspect of the strategy and not the "think" part. The administrators may say that "the teacher was doing a think-pair-share as a collaborative structure." They may even indicate that *they liked* that the teacher was using a TPS because it deviates from the lecture in the last scenario. When asked: *How much think-time did students get and how do you know?* The answers vary from "none" to "I'm not sure." In this case, the teacher may be doing a pair-share, but lost all of the cognitive and preparatory value in think-time that should have been provided in the accurate use of the strategy.

These are clear examples of what some leaders learn to notice within minutes, even seconds, of visiting a classroom and what others simply miss. The difference can be seen in the quality of the feedback that's provided for the teacher as well as any subsequent improvements to performance. We can set all of the KPIs in the world—to improve math scores or increase student talk time—but if we don't use our Six-Step Practical Change Model that helps us to lead with a DTV, we won't see changes at the classroom level that will lead to new outcomes. If we don't have a clear vision through to the model that we expect everyone to implement as a change to what was previously done, we can't provide specific feedback to teachers that addresses the nuances in their precision with the new instructional practices. When our focus and determination aren't clear enough to change beliefs and behaviors, nothing changes. When nothing changes, nothing changes.

Reflection Questions

1. What big ideas of DTV resonate with you? Why?

2. Think of a time when you or someone else lost the big picture as in the Whac-a-Mole Leadership Problem that we described. How might a DTV using the Six-Step Practical Change Model have helped?

3. Which of the six steps in our model for DTV needs the most attention in your school?

4. How might sharpening your noticing skills as a leader impact teaching and learning in the classroom?

MINDSHIFT #6: LEADING WITH A "YES, AND" ATTITUDE

> Life is not consisted only of "yes" and "no," but a lot of "yes and" and "no but."
>
> —Vann Chow (2016)

 Outside Story: Netflix and Will

"That will never work," are words Marc Randolph's wife said about the idea he and his friend, Reed Hastings, had (Randolph, 2019). Randolph later used these same words as the title of his book that tells the success story of one of the world's most iconic companies. Thanks to Randolph and Hastings, the way we rent and view movies has forever changed. It's become simpler, more convenient, more diverse, and, not to mention, quite lucrative for the Netflix founders.

On their commute to work, the friends brainstormed many possibilities for a startup company. They dismissed personalized shampoo, surfboards, and even dog food formulated specifically for individual dogs before Randolph suggested an online video store. In 1997, most video stores were stocking VHS (Video Home System) tapes and renting them for $3 per night. The thought of using an Internet-based rental system that relied on the US postal system to deliver the movies sparked Hasting's attention.

The first major obstacle was the cost of sending clunky VHS tapes in the mail without enormous shipping fees. They shifted their thinking to sending Digital Video Discs (DVDs) through the mail. New to the market, DVDs posed a few new problems. One, not every household had a DVD player, two, they were initially expensive, and three, not every movie was even available on DVD at the time. This trifecta of barriers would have shut down most people, putting the concept of Netflix in the trash alongside customized dog food. Instead, the friends used the obstacles as inspiration to make their idea even better. The first step they took was to determine if the DVDs could be mailed. Because music CDs were the same size as DVDs, they tested their plan by mailing the CD in a business envelope and sending it to Reed's home. It arrived in perfectly usable condition.

The VHS-by-mail plan morphed quickly into the world's first DVD-by-mail company. They offered stock for 50 cents a share. Reed Hastings and Marc Randolph struggled to get investors, but despite the repeated encounters with naysayers, they persisted and addressed obstacles to pave a bumpy path to success. Their consistent focus on their goal and their will to solve a problem led the team to overcome negativity and the lack of faith from others. Determination and a worthwhile goal, sprinkled with calculated and researched risk, paid off. Today, the once 50-cent share costs nearly five hundred dollars. So much for what thousands of investors thought would be a flop.

 Flawed Thinking: The "Yeah, But" Barrier

In the previous chapters, we have outlined why we struggle to see and act on different chronic problems and explored the various barriers that prevent school leaders from defining, identifying, and properly analyzing their problems.

Whether caused by an expert blind spot (Chapter 5) or one's inability to unveil the complexities of an issue (Chapter 4), school decision-makers too often stumble through the first steps of tackling perennial problems. And yet another barrier presents itself—our tendency to fall face first into the "yeah, but" pit. In this chapter, we tackle flawed thinking by showing how to use a decision-making process to willingly go down the less traveled road with the security of well-defined tools. The right tools, along with the right mindshift, are necessary to systematically explore viable options for solving problems.

INFAMOUS "YEAH, BUTS"

Netflix is far from the only example to benefit from "Yes, And" thinking that was applied to produce a better product, service, or outcome. Look at Figure 6.1 for more examples of how infamous "yeah, buts" were faced with "Yes, And" thinking, which provided positive results.

6.1 Infamous "Yeah, Buts" Turned to "Yes, Ands"

Infamous "Yeah, But"	Result of "Yes, And" Thinking
In 1985, a *New York Times* article deemed the laptop a dead computer tool. The article claimed that cost, size, and general user interest in being attached to a keyboard were prohibitive (Sandberg-Diment, 1985).	Laptops continue to be lighter, smaller, and more powerful. In 2025, 272 million laptops are forecast to be shipped (Alsop, 2022).
The iPhone was met with several naysayers who thought it would "crash in flames" and many would regret ditching their Blackberries (Sin, 2017).	Steve Jobs' obsession with gathering his top people to curate the very best ideas fueled creativity and inspiration from his workers (Schwantes, 2019). It is argued that without smartphones, businesses like Uber or apps like Venmo wouldn't even exist (Hartmans, 2018).

(Continued)

6.1 (Continued)

Infamous "Yeah, But"	Result of "Yes, And" Thinking
As the *Literary Digest* reported in 1899, cost was a main factor for the automobile to be viewed as impractical, stating "it will never, of course, come into as common use as the bicycle" (Whigham, 2016).	Henry Ford created the assembly line, which allowed for mass production of automobiles. This brought the price down, and automobiles are the main source of transportation in the United States today.

The "Yes, And" outcomes described in Figure 6.1 were the result of a mindshift to determination, problem-solving, and a dogged pursuit to succeed. To see results and work toward achieving success, the power of self- and collective efficacy must be present, especially, when confronted with "impossible" obstacles and a lack of belief from our closest colleagues, friends, and partners.

"Yeah, but" is a trap, an endless hole of limitations imposed by failure to see possibilities. This is not to say that every idea is good or that every business will succeed. According to the US Bureau of Labor Statistics, in 2019 close to 800,000 businesses were started, and, of those, roughly 20 percent are projected to fail in their first two years (BLS, 2021). The ones who make it, will have done so with a willingness to continue to pursue the possibilities and to walk down the path of uncertainty. They'll take risks, knowing that without the trek of a path less traveled there is no chance of finding something new.

FEAR, COMPLAINING, AND MIMICRY

Chapter 3 described how using a beginner's mind widens thinking about a situation that is familiar so that we are able to see it with curiosity and a newfound interest. When someone's expertise prohibits them from seeing the needs of the situation or individual, essentially blocking the ability to see a scenario with fresh eyes, it's called an *expert blind spot* (Nathan, Koedinger, & Alibali, n.d.). The "yeah, but" reaction could be spawned from that same experience. As perennial problems persist, educators can grow to accept them as the norm. The tolerance to an old problem becoming or has already become a crisis fosters the blind spot and makes it easier to throw down a "yeah, but" rather than face a potential change.

Fear of change is a predisposition of humans, and resistance is often the product. Our brains prefer consistency and routine over the unknown. Think of a time when someone suggested that you take an unfamiliar route to get to your destination, and you thought (or even said), "I'll just go my way, even if it takes a little longer"; this is a classic example of sticking with what's known and comfortable. It's often the fear of the uncharted path that causes a person to resist change. It's not a personality flaw; it's the way we are wired, and, in many instances, it's beneficial because it's designed to protect us. Dr. David Rock and Dr. Al H. Ringleb, neuroscientists and authors of *Handbook of Neuroleadership* (2013), liken the fear of the unknown, which is triggered by the thought of change, to fear of failure. It registers in our brains similarly to how we process an error. It provokes a sense of danger and creates an unsafe feeling. Because the brain goes into an alert state when fear is triggered, it makes a person want to avoid the experience altogether. The thought of tackling unresolved issues inherently requires change, which increases alertness and elicits resistance. A person might subconsciously offer "yeah, buts" as a defense mechanism to avoid the potential of change and the possibility of failure, even if they generally have optimistic outlooks.

Other neuroscience around the "yeah, but" mindset is linked to complaining (Bradberry, 2016). If you've ever felt better after ranting about something just to get it off your chest, then you can relate. Cortisol is a stress hormone that, when released, shifts you into the fight or flight mode. When your brain is sent into this state of mind, it curbs nonessential functions for survival and increases your attentiveness. The purpose is to help you identify a threat and determine how to keep yourself safe. It triggers parts of the brain that control mood and motivation. Therefore, when cortisol is flowing, you are not in your most thoughtful, resourceful, or open state of mind.

To make matters worse, complaining, or frequently offering "yeah, but" responses, can be addictive and contagious. Your brain's primary function is to keep you alive. This clever organ conserves energy through efficiency. Therefore, it creates wires in the brain whenever behaviors are repeated to make them easier to access in the future. Negativity is no exception. Every time a person complains, the synapses get closer together and more easily trigger the "yeah, but" type of thinking.

> If we are going to resolve issues in education that have lingered for far too long, a crisis mindset will need to notice "yeah, buts" in any form and combat them with a mindshift and a new phrase.

Additionally, research has shown that people attempt to mimic the emotions, movements, and other facets of those around them through *limbic synchrony* (Goman, 2011). This can be helpful when trying to be empathic, but when trying to uncover roadblocks and determine potential solutions, a mob of educators mirroring "yeah, buts" is not likely to lead to productive solutions for old problems.

The "yeah, but" mentality might be more suggested. In addition to "yeah, but" you might hear flawed thinking in comments or questions like these:

- That will never be successful.

- We'd have to do X in order for it to work, which is not possible.

- How would we handle [insert obstacle]?

- What about [insert barrier]?
- Then we'd have to...
- That's not our decision...
- [Name or organization] would have to be on board.
- That will take too long.
- How would we do that?
- It can't be done.
- We've tried that before, and it didn't work.

Regardless of why the "yeah, buts" start to surface, the bottom line is they prematurely eliminate ideas and diminish innovation and risk-taking. If we are going to resolve issues in education that have lingered for far too long, a crisis mindset will need to notice "yeah, buts" in any form and combat them with a mindshift and a new phrase. Leaders need a new response that will welcome a list of challenges, one that invites solutions, and a frame of mind that focuses on productive discourse that leads to quality action plans to finally rid education of the many crises we face.

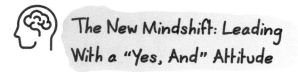

The New Mindshift: Leading With a "Yes, And" Attitude

Unlike going down a "yeah, but" chasm, the "Yes, And" Attitude embraces the process of out-of-the-box thinking, outlandish ideas, and innovation. This approach accepts anything proposed and explores any road necessary, especially those less traveled. A "Yes, And" Attitude *is a way of confronting roadblocks, issues, and obstacles and believing that there is a way around them.*

MODEL: DEFINE, ANALYZE, IDENTIFY, SELECT, DEVELOP, IMPLEMENT, AND EVALUATE

Problem-solving and decision-making are multistep processes that take a person or group through a series of cognitive reflections to help determine the best course of action. Our representation of full-circle decision-making is provided in Figure 6.2. The most vital aspect of the process is to ensure that the entire journey is mapped out. Narrowing in on solutions prematurely disrupts proper problem-solving and creates a symptoms-based approach. Following the steps outlined is critical to determining if the efforts are making a difference.

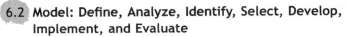

6.2 Model: Define, Analyze, Identify, Select, Develop, Implement, and Evaluate

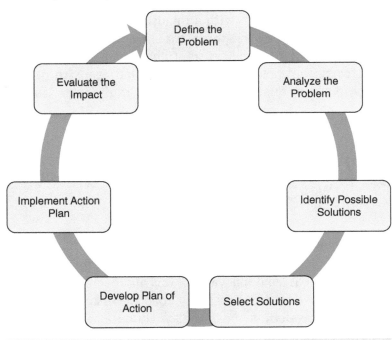

Phase 1: Define the Problem

When making decisions to solve old problems, we first have to get clarity on the real issue and the underlying symptoms. Leaders who dig deeply to find root causes for problems are better positioned to counter them and prevent them from recurring. A method like the 5 Whys technique, developed by Toyota founder, Sakichi Toyoda (George, Rowlands, Price, & Maxey, 2004), is a simple approach to drilling deep into a problem. As its title suggests, the team simply asks "why" repeatedly. After the first why is asked, the second "why" digs more deeply into the first response. Figure 6.3 shows the progression that leads to a root cause.

Phase 2: Analyze the Problem

In Phase 2, leaders explore all of the complexities within a problem. In this part of the decision-making model, we uncover all the related arms through the Octopus Approach (see Chapter 4). This might mean going back and forth between Phase 1 and 2 to identify relevant components and find the root causes for each of them.

Phase 3: Identify All Possible Solutions

Look again at Figure 6.2, we are setting our sights on the action that takes us from Phase 2, Analyze the Problem, to Phase 3, Identify Possible Solutions. Let's assume, for the

6.3 5 Whys Technique

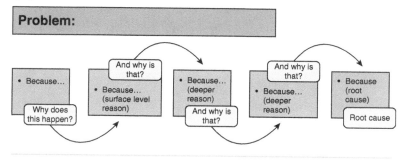

purposes of this chapter, that an administrative team is tackling an ongoing issue in a school. They have thoroughly defined and analyzed the situation. Root causes are identified, and the arms of the octopus were sufficiently investigated. In short, the team has clarity on the problem, and it's time to take the next step.

That next leap in the problem-solving process is Phase 3: Identify All Possible Solutions. Unlike Mr. Frost, whose road only diverged into two paths, schools are often not so fortunate. There are typically multiple "roads" to consider when solving an old problem that has become a crisis in a school. So many, in fact, that it's typical for folx to settle on the most common or readily available, dwindling them down quickly to move on to the fourth problem-solving phase and choose a solution. This urge to charge ahead is a breeding ground for "yeah, but" thinking. Ideas are shot down before they have legs. Granted, the actual words may be "We've tried that..." or "Won't that require...?" or "The staff is burnt out..." but the impact is the same: "**Yeah**, nice idea, **but** that won't work!" Once the ping-ponging begins, it's hard to stop, and potentially great ideas and solutions never see the light of day.

There is a reason that the third problem-solving phase is separate from the fourth. The point is to brainstorm before judging if an idea is better than another or if it's plausible at all. The "yeah, buts" come from every angle and quickly. Yeah, but that "costs too much," or "it would take too long," "the community won't go for it," "we tried that before," or even no explanation at all, just a general belief and attitude that something won't work. When "yeah, buts" are given power to remove an idea from the table before it has been explored, our likelihood of solving the problem becomes limited. Leaders can avoid this potential blackhole by honoring the "Yes, And" Attitude by giving Phase 3 the team's full attention.

Phase 4: Select a Solution

Once the team has a list of possible solutions that have been generated without vetting, it's time to select a solution. As the team considers all the possibilities along with available resources, you will want to maintain a "Yes, And" Attitude as options are discussed and prioritized. The most viable solution might not be the best one. "Yeah, but" thinking has the potential to lead the team to the easiest, least confrontational, or quickest solution. Be sure to continue to embrace obstacles with your "Yes, And" Attitude until the solution that surfaces is the one that will finally put the old problem you're addressing to rest. We stand our greatest chance of solving these persistent problems if we don't shy away from challenges within the right solution by applying "Yes, And" thinking in every phase of the decision-making process.

Phase 5: Develop a Plan of Action

Once you have your solution, a plan of action should be drawn out. Phase 5 includes creating a step-by-step plan designed with strategies and associated activities. This is a perfect part of the decision-making cycle to focus on Leading with a Disciplined Tunnel Vision, as discussed in the previous chapter. The purpose for the action plan is to make changes in order to avoid these old problems from becoming permanent factors that impede student success.

Phase 6: Implement the Plan of Action

We all have examples of strategic plans that look great on paper and do a fine job of filling a three-ring binder and taking up space on our shelves. "Yes, And" leaders follow up with Phase 6 and help the plan get off the ground and into implementation. Concrete phases of implementation help break it into parts so supports and resources can be gathered while key personnel are identified to guide each step of implementation. Your Battleground Mentality will bring a relentless, experimental, agile, and learning culture to life as your plan plays out in this phase and in Phase 7.

Phase 7: Evaluate the Impact

Finding new ways to think about old problems is in many ways uncharted thinking territory. True, that the problems have been around since most of us can remember, but thinking about them in new ways makes the outcome of solutions unknown. Therefore, we contend that Phase 7: Evaluate the Impact is more important when applying mindshifts than in a typical school improvement process. While any plan of action should have an evaluative component, it is particularly important when the need to readjust is likely. Another octopus tentacle might pop up once your implementation begins. If so, use your "Yes, And" Attitude to embrace the issue that emerges and initiate the decision-making process again to address it. If you design and apply formative and summative assessments associated with key performance indicators to measure progress along the way, you will have a complete system for applying "Yes, And" to your lingering school problems.

BENEFITS OF "YES, AND" FULL-CIRCLE DECISION-MAKING

When the "yeah, but" voices are given authority to dismiss solutions before a decision-making model completes its cycle, the school runs the risk of becoming a culture of "yeah, buts" and negativity, limiting progress. This isn't to generalize that people who present barriers aren't well intentioned. There's a place to scrutinize potential solutions and identify roadblocks. However, if brainstorming and "yeah, butting" occur simultaneously, the "yeah, buts" will consume every idea, and the best solution might get squashed in the same moment that it's shared. The primary reason for this type of "yeah, butting" is a lack of attention paid to Full-Circle Decision-Making in attending to each aspect of the circle as its own step. The movement from one step to another without spending the time needed to exhaust all of our options stems from a culture of fear, our addiction to complaining, and the ways in which we mimic bad behavior.

WHAT COMEDIANS CAN TEACH US

The Second City is perhaps the most famous comedy training center in the world. Tim Meadows, Tina Fey, Stephen Colbert, Joan Rivers, Eugene Levy, and Bill Murray are among the alumni of this prestigious comedy school. There are seven elements of improvisation that The Second City teaches. They include strategies that support collaboration, supporting your fellow teammates and listening, and learning and recovering from failure. But before they jump into these areas, The Second City students learn the "Yes, And" Attitude. It is introduced on day one of their very first class.

The message in a comedy scene is to acknowledge what your acting partner sets up with a "yes." Then, build on the scene to make it more entertaining for the audience with your "and." Their classes not only support aspiring actors to be funnier, but the training center also supports public speakers, businesspeople, and even teachers. Skills like "Yes, And" taught at The Second City are tools that can be used in life too (Leonard & Yorton, 2015). To learn more about each of the seven elements of The Second City improvisation course, search online for "Improv Comedy in the Workplace" by David Grissom (2017).

We are not suggesting that you approach a crisis as an improv, although humor and laughter are linked to "creativity and ideation" (Ma, 2014). If leaders desire to take hold of problems that are important, urgent, and persistent, they will need the skills that widen perspectives, broaden leadership, and persevere when faced with uncertainty and failure. The comedians, teachers, and leaders at The Second City have already figured this out. Similar to Netflix founders Randolph and Hastings, the goal is always in the forefront, and the desire to succeed is paramount. On the path to finding new ways to think about old problems, "Yes, And" takes leaders a step closer while "yeah, but" sends us a step backwards.

The Urban Dictionary (2019) lists *yeahbut* and *yabut* as words used when in a hurry to argue. People described as "yeah, buts" are thought to be unpleasable and vocal with their negativity about situations, often interrupting. As mentioned earlier in the chapter, consistently addressing issues from a deficit position, and looking for reasons why progress cannot be made, develops a mentality that perpetuates perennial problems.

It takes more than swapping "but" for "and" to solve an issue. The semantics serve as a conduit to a mindshift. The composition of "yeah, but" and "Yes, And" look similar from a grammatical perspective. An affirmative is followed by a conjunction. The difference is the impact "yeah, but" has on a person's idea for resolving a perennial problem. When "Yes, And" is offered in its place, the tone morphs. "Yeah" is dismissive. "Yes" is acknowledging. "But" attempts to end a conversation topic while "and" seeks to explore and deepen it. Figure 6.4 offers a comparison of the two mentalities.

6.4   The "Yeah, But" Versus "Yes, And" Mentality

Yeah, But	Yes, And
Attempts to shut down ideas	Acknowledges barriers for the purpose of minimizing or overcoming them
Often leads to closure	Keeps conversation open and unfinished
Identifies roadblocks are reasons why a problem cannot be solved	Reveals potential obstacles and finds a way to overcome them so that they do not prevent future progress
Sabotages positive progress	Evades sabotage by directly addressing potential issues
All or nothing attitude	Leaves room for modification and innovation

Applying a "Yes, And" Attitude to Homelessness and Discipline

The mindshift to a "Yes, And" Attitude is ultimately changing the perspective you have as you lead teams in problem-solving. Inevitably real problems will emerge, unplanned obstacles will surface, and the way you respond to them will determine if you're applying a "yeah, but" or "Yes, And" mentality. There will be times when the solution seems out of reach. Perhaps the perspective seems beyond the grips of K–12 education. Leaders who apply a "Yes, And" Attitude help their team embrace and ultimately overcome old problems that might otherwise seem hopeless. Let's see how this new mindshift connects to homelessness and discipline.

MAKING THE CONNECTION: STUDENT HOMELESSNESS IN SCHOOLS

There are examples in education when a "Yes, And" Attitude has brought about mandated change that forced districts to embrace reality and put structures in place to minimize circumstances that might be detrimental to student success. For example, according to the National Center for Homeless Education (NCHE), in the 2019–20 school year, 2.5 percent of all students enrolled in public schools experienced homelessness. That's nearly 1.3 million children in America. Even more troubling is that students of color are disproportionately experiencing homelessness than their white peers (NCHE, 2021).

Rather than apply a "yeah, but" mentality to homelessness by limiting a school's role to support all children during school hours, the McKinney Homeless Assistance Act was signed in 1987 by President Ronald Reagan and then renamed to McKinney-Vento Act by Bill Clinton in 2000 expanded how schools assist students and families. The legislation requires schools to apply a "Yes, And" thought process so educators could create systems to guarantee that schools would consider homelessness in their schools and develop ways to minimize the impact that homelessness has on student success (NCHE, 2021). The vision of the legislation was to go from *"yeah,* homelessness is a problem, *but* there's nothing we can do about it" and shift to *"yes,* homelessness is a problem, *and* we have to do something about it."

Legislation alone is not the solution to shifting from "yeah, but" thinking to leading with a "Yes, And" Attitude. Governmental mandates, like McKinney-Vento, simply call attention to issues that hinder student learning and growth. It is still the local districts and their thinking around the problem that determine if an obstacle becomes a barrier or if the school will determine how to counteract the impact it has on progress. The solution is not "yes, and somebody else should do something about it." Recognizing issues that prevent success and owning the responsibility to find solutions that permit success despite the existing challenges as a school community are the attitudes of "Yes, And" leaders.

One organization, Kids' Food Basket, in Grand Rapids Michigan has been leading its community with a "Yes, And" Attitude. The organization provides approximately 9,300 meals every day to kids and families. If this weren't loud enough "YES, students are hungry after school, AND we can provide meals for them and their families," the organization continued to search for other barriers to embrace and overcome with this mindshift. Bridget Clark Whitney, President and CEO, shared the organization's effort to combat racial, economic, and systemic barriers to food equity. They reapplied a "Yes, And" Attitude by teaching students home gardening skills, connecting them with community resources, and helping them to establish and maintain healthy lifestyle habits. The impact of leading with a "Yes, And" Attitude enabled Kids' Food Basket to feed more than 1.3 million meals in 2021 to families, and the organization earned national recognition by the US Department of Agriculture.

When student learning is influenced by outside factors, applying a "Yes, And" Attitude empowers school leaders to follow full-circle decision-making and accept the challenges that come with tackling old problems. If we are going to find a way to rethink issues like homelessness, student discipline, school readiness, and other educational crises, this mindshift is essential. Yes, living conditions and lack of basic needs impact students' abilities to focus on learning. Yes, this reality is not caused by the school district. Yes, homelessness is a systemic problem in the United States. The next necessary line signifies whether or not we're leading with a crisis mindset, one that sees the urgency and importance of solving this persistent problem. It starts with "And."

MAKING THE CONNECTION: SCHOOL DISCIPLINE

Another education connection that often spins its "yeah, but" wheels without moving forward to solving the problem is managing student behavior in schools. A Gallup study revealed that 46 percent of teachers report high daily stress during the school year and among the main sources of that stress is student behavior problems (Gallup, 2014). Far too many adults rely on a punitive approach when faced with discipline issues, and still our discipline issues persist. You would think that given what we know, which will be discussed more in the next chapter, any solution would be welcomed. The reality is that schools are slow to shift away from old thinking that bestows punitive consequences in hopes that the punishment alone will teach them a lesson and change their behavior when they return to class.

This "yeah, but" flawed thinking focuses on predetermined negative consequences when school expectations are violated. It assumes that the threat of a punishment alone will deter a child or adolescent from acting out. However, this belief simply isn't supported. First, children and adolescents have underdeveloped frontal lobes, which is the rational, decision-making part of the brain. The assumption that youngsters purposefully consider their actions prior to making them is most often invalid. The common response "You should have thought about that before you. . ." serves as evidence that the disciplinarian holds some belief that students have the skills to be mindful in an emotional moment, analyze outcomes, and make a thoughtful decision. Not true.

Not only does a punitive approach to student discipline not work for many students, but it is also harmful to the student-adult relationship and sets a "gotcha culture" in the classroom and school. Sending a student to detention for coming to class unprepared for the tenth time or suspending a student for bullying rarely alters behavior. Although separating an aggressor from their victim may be helpful, removing the bully from school for one to three days does nothing to repair the harm already done or set the victim's mind at ease that they will be safe from being targeted again in the future. What's missing is a "Yes, And" Attitude to align the behavior with a consequence that focuses on the harm that was caused and plan to repair it.

Leaders who have made this mindshift already understand that "yeah, but" thinking leads to establishing blame, guilt, and using shaming and stigmatizing as the go-to response for undesired behavior. They know the attention, as with most "yeah, but" mentalities, focuses on what has happened in the past as well as a set of penalties that are viewed as "deserved." Therefore, they have implemented a restorative approach to many discipline situations that their teachers and leaders face daily. The approach is more about how to acknowledge what happened and focus on how to avoid repeating the behavior and consequently the negative outcomes it creates (Maynard & Weinstein, 2019). With this future-focused, empathetic perspective, different questions emerge (White, 2012):

1. What happened?

2. What were you thinking at the time?

3. What have you thought about since?

4. Who or what has been affected by what you have done?

5. In what way have they been affected?

6. What do you think you need to do to make things right?

As suggested in the Fix School Discipline Toolkit (2014), it might mean teaching a set of coping skills, identifying the root causes for the behavior to lessen triggers, or shedding a more relational light on how individual choices impact others, encouraging empathy and care.

The "Yes, And" Attitude of approaching discipline from a restorative perspective doesn't condone the behavior. The "yes" is not an approval. It is an acknowledgment of what occurred and a desire to understand and address it, not dismiss it. Look at Figure 6.5 to see the shift in tone that "Yes, And" brings to the situation.

The "and" is an addition to the experience for everyone involved in the effort to deal with it directly. This chapter is not about how to implement restorative practices, there are plenty of resources available for that, such as the International Institute for Restorative Practices and Hacking School Discipline by Maynard and Weinstein. Using Restorative Practices to solve discipline problems is provided as an example of an old problem in education that, with a new mindshift, might be solved. Yes,

6.5 "Yes, And" Tone

Yeah or Yes	But Attitude	And Attitude
You're having a bad day	but that is no reason to take it out on your teacher.	and we have to find better outlets than taking it out on your teacher.
You didn't finish your project	but you have known about this assignment for weeks.	and you could use some help with time management.
You got some bad news	but it's time to focus on math.	and you're probably going to have trouble focusing on math.

our discipline practices are punitive and are not improving the culture. Yes, some students feel threatened by their class-mates. Yes, students do not believe they have a trusting adult in the school. Yes, we have repeat offenders who don't seem impacted by suspensions. Yes-Yes-Yes, *and* we are making the mindshift to find a solution anyway.

 ## Technical Tip: Let Go of "No"

The popular children's book *Yes Day!* by Amy Krause Rosenthal was published in 2009, way before Jennifer Garner starred in the 2021 movie version (Arteta, 2021). The story walks through an entire day where a set of parents say "yes" to their children's requests. There are some guidelines, including a budget, nothing illegal, and safety first, but nearly everything is fair game, for one day. The message was not just a comic relief for readers and movie-goers. Parenting blogs, talk shows, and journal articles all flooded their audiences with activities, templates, ideas, and samples so families across America could join the fun and invite their children to enjoy their own Yes Day.

Acceptance of an idea without judgment was freeing for the adult characters. Letting go of "no" and not having to decide if a request would be granted or not was part of the reprieve they felt by not having to dismiss anything. The characters were challenged from time to time. Years of saying no in the spirit of protecting their children didn't just vanish. And because of the normal knee-jerk "no," it took practice to learn to say "yes."

To prepare you to counteract "yeah, buts" with "Yes, And," try practicing mini "yes days." The first step is to say "yes" more often. Choose an aspect of your life and make an effort to say yes to everything. Even if you have to qualify your yes, just the immediate "yes" will get you some yeses under your belt so that you will be more likely to apply the "Yes, And" Attitude when it's needed. Figure 6.6 offers a few examples for how you can change the narrative without sacrificing the message.

6.6 Language Shift to Yes

Request	No Response	Yes Response
I want a piece of cake.	No, you haven't finished your dinner yet.	Yes, as soon as your dinner is finished.
May I go to the park?	No, I need you to watch your sister.	Yes, if you take your sister with you.
Do you have a pencil I can borrow?	No, I never get them back.	Yes, your phone charger will serve as good collateral.

With a bit of effort and some practice, your default responses might eventually become "yes." The next step is to start building "and" into your regular vocabulary. Make an effort to replace "but" with "and." Listen to how much kinder "and" sounds by reading the following passages aloud.

- I appreciate the offer of cookies AND I'm trying to reduce my sugar intake.

- You have a reasonable request AND my budget is depleted.

- Your concern is valid AND I think we should consider. . . .

- I'd love to participate AND I have other plans tonight.

- I see your point AND I'd like to think about it.

- Your lesson was great AND there is one area for you to think about.

- I know you would like to speak to me AND I have another appointment right now.

In *Getting to Yes: Negotiating Agreement Without Giving In*, Ury and Fisher (2011) eloquently describe the importance of focusing on the "interests" of a group or person and not their "position" on a matter. This helps avoid right and wrong or yes and no as finite aspects of a conversation so the best possible answer is always pursued, which is in the best "interest" of everyone.

Letting go of "no" is a way to build a "Yes, And" Attitude.

Letting go of "no" is a way to build a "Yes, And" Attitude. It's not isolated to home or school. The more accepting and positive tone that saying yes creates will set the scene for more productive thinking that leads to solution-based thinking. In order to solve perennial problems in education, a "Yes, And" Attitude is necessary to explore solutions that have yet to be put into action. As we will highlight in the next chapter, the "and" within your mindshift doesn't have to require reinventing the wheel. Many times, strategies have already been researched and proven effective, it just takes a leader who is willing to use a "Yes, And" Attitude to take action.

Reflection Questions

1. Which aspects of the Full-Circle Decision-Making model does your team need to spend more time with? What would it look like to implement that step in your next meeting? What thinking or planning might you need to do ahead of time to make it successful?

2. How does a "Yes, And" Attitude add to, align with, or conflict from your current thinking about problem-solving?

3. What would be the biggest benefits to adopting a "Yes, And" Attitude in your school or district? In what ways might it impact the culture?

4. Think of three different teams in your school or district. How might you introduce the "Yes, And" Attitude to each of those teams?

7

MINDSHIFT #7: LEADING WITH A "GO WITH WHAT IS KNOWN" RESPONSE

Think analytically, rigorously, and systematically about a business problem and come up with a solution that leverages the available data.

—Michael O'Connell (2012)

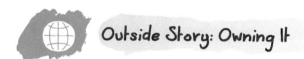

Outside Story: Owning It

Decision-making is a prerequisite skill for leadership. It's not easy, though. Uncertainty, doubt, resistance, and complacency can stop anyone from making necessary changes for improvement. It is the risk that every action carries that weighs so heavily on decision-makers. Leaders who effectively manage risk, we love to herald for their courage and leaps of faith, and for good reason. We admire their acumen and resilience; the Everest-size challenges they overcome, when the risk is too great for others, inspire us as we turn the pages of *Bloomberg Businessweek* or *Forbes*, yearning to understand the ingredients of their prosperity.

Although the conditions of success aren't always the same, there are key factors that indicate a business is about to meet its demise. Unstable leadership, loss of profit share, poor reputation, and a host of other signals can reveal a company's descent. In 2009, Domino's Pizza faced a crisis. As former CEO Patrick Doyle said, "When we did consumer tests, if they knew the pizza was Domino's, they actually liked it less than if they just thought it was a random unbranded pizza." Further comments including that their "pizza tasted like cardboard" and that the "sauce tasted like ketchup" presented real issues for the company (Haden, 2021). As consumers, we have seen companies fight the uphill battle of refuting the public sentiments in an attempt to explain their way out of dismal data. In the case of Domino's executives, their response was risky and courageous.

The Domino's executives didn't push back on the feedback they heard from the public. Instead, they embraced the condemning messages, listened to their consumers, and prepared to save their pizza company. They publicly apologized and admitted their wrongs, committed to serve people better. The message was genuine, heartfelt, and what is viewed in the business world as incredibly risky. The greater risk, however, was implementing sales and marketing tactics that shied away from what they knew. People didn't like Domino's pizza and a catchy jingle or new packaging was unlikely to alter that undeniable fact.

Not only did they make the necessary ingredient changes, but knowing something drastic had to be done, the company wasn't sheepish about what everyone already knew. They followed the Mark Cuban (2015) line of thinking, "...if you're prepared and you know what it takes, it's not a risk. You just have to figure out how to get there. There's always a way to get there." Domino's got busy revamping their pizza recipes, and they exploited their dire situation by having real customers express their dissatisfaction on commercials. Their entire marketing campaign was built on one message: "We hear you."

Even though it was uncomfortable and unpredictable, admitting that they weren't serving their customers well was not as big of a risk as it might seem because that opinion was already widespread. They went with what was known and trusted; their transparency to communicate that they were more committed to fixing the problem than covering it up would pay off. They still made pizza, just much better. They still delivered pizza, just more efficiently. Their core business didn't change but how they did it drastically improved. They understood the harsh reality that the data were telling them, they swallowed the criticism whole, and then made significant changes. Today, Domino's has fully rebounded. Some would say it was miraculous. We say it was a Go With What You Know Attitude.

 ## Flawed Thinking: The Untouchables

Intentionally listening to those within the school community, tuning into the issues and challenges within a school is ponderous but necessary. Willingly accepting, confronting, and working to alter areas of poor performance, although complex, is the call of a school leader. Unfortunately, it doesn't come naturally. In fact, we are wired to do the opposite. We love great inspirational stories, quotes, and quips that invigorate and restore us, such as the advice to fail forward, trust your intuition, or, one of our favorites from Henry Van Dyke, "Some people succeed because they are destined to, but most people succeed because they are determined to."

Tolstoy (1993) said, "When in doubt, my dear fellow, do nothing." Unfortunately, doing nothing comes at a great cost to our schools.

This mountain of inspirational quotes and ideas are needed because we function more closely to what Tolstoy (1993) said, "When in doubt, my dear fellow, do nothing." Unfortunately, doing nothing comes at a great cost to our schools. Throughout this book, we've identified flawed thinking that hampers school success: not focusing on the most important areas of schooling, the educational system itself, expert blind spots, limited tunnel vision, resistance to change, and in this chapter, those areas free from criticism, the untouchables, as we call them, and the doubt that seeps in when we're unsure of ourselves.

DOUBT-FILLED THINKING

Doubt is a vice, and familiarity tightens its grip. Our beloved instructional practices, initiatives, and programs, some of the most common and familiar, are often outdated and ineffective; yet we hold onto them as if they were sacred, unwilling to abandon them and replace them with something superior. We allow doubt, which is regularly revealed through inaction, to prevent progress. Doubt severely hampers our willingness to believe our data sources and the research to which we have access to prompt necessary changes. Fortunately, for Domino's, Doyle and the executives didn't let the untouchables or doubt-filled thinking persuade them into making conventional marketing decisions that most likely would have resulted in meager efforts, limited change, and the demise of the pizza chain.

Let's explore these protected untouchables. It's important to understand that each school has its own initiatives, ideas, and programs that are near and dear to everyone's hearts. Those things that are immune to question, opposition, or critique. If you dispute the existence of untouchables in your school, just start a conversation in the teacher's lounge about student dress code. Underestimating someone's belief in something is a mistake leaders cannot make. This is where the balance between the art and science of leadership is important. Possessing both elements enables administrators to be prepared to confront the level of resistance they will encounter with the right information, supported by the right approach.

Underestimating someone's belief in something is a mistake leaders cannot make.

UNCHALLENGED BELIEFS

One of the most damning untouchables isn't a thing but rather a belief—a belief that all ideas, initiatives, and strategies are of equal value and effectiveness. This outlook crushes change and progress. Literacy is considered a fundamental skill that all schools should actively focus on. Under the umbrella of literacy, we find reading, writing, language, speaking, and listening. Schools often embark on initiatives such as *reading across the curriculum* to improve reading scores. The challenge doesn't lie within the goal to embed reading strategies into other content areas, but, rather, at the implementation level. Without the proper guidance, support, and direction, teachers will default to practices that are easy to manage like Drop Everything and Read or round robin reading. Round robin reading remains popular even though the research and data reveal its limitations (Grifhorst, Lessway, & Zamborowski, 2012). This not only limits student gains in reading across the curriculum, but will spend invaluable time on a strategy that won't work. As Elizabeth Brinkerhoff and Alysia Roehrig write, "We have to be fully aware of ineffective practices and 'timewasters' that don't support effective instructional practices" (Brinkerhoff & Roehrig, 2014).

This dovetails into our second mistake, which is not using research to guide instructional decisions with surgical accuracy. There are several strategies we hold onto, protect, and argue over in spite of evidence that details their degrees of effectiveness. Lecturing, class size, and technology are just a few examples of ideas and strategies that continue to be hotly debated or heralded as an all-encompassing fix. Consider one of the ultimate sacred activities: homework. Homework is often used incorrectly and does not support student learning as teachers believe it should (Capek Tingley, n.d.). Yet, if you want to spark passionate dialogue at any table, bring up the use of homework as an instructional strategy during a department meeting.

In *Hacking Homework: 10 Strategies That Inspire Learning Outside the Classroom* (2016) Starr Sackstein and Connie Hamilton point out that when you listen closely to supporters who routinely assign homework, you'll notice that their arguments turn away from learning and shift to student responsibility. The conversation doesn't reference the data and the effect size of homework, or even the needed support and resources at home. Rather it quickly turns to student behavior—laziness, effort, and motivation. The pushback ignores the logic that homework doesn't teach responsibility; it expects students to be responsible and then punishes them when they're not (Sackstein & Hamilton, 2016).

Unfortunately, these discussions can turn into heated debates that reveal people's value systems and social attitudes rather than the data and research on the practice. Therefore, it's vital for school leaders to be comfortable challenging pervasive but ineffective aspects of schooling. Let's revisit Doyle and Domino's executive team. We applaud their success after the fact, but imagine what the conversations were like internally when the company was failing. In the face of discouraging information, lame excuses, defensiveness, and denial must have occurred, encompassing every conversation from net profit margins to the quality of their products.

This is how the untouchables in education must be challenged—evidence, research, and doggedness toward masterful implementation. It is the implementation where the nuances live, and the only place where we realize positive changes. If we are going to challenge the sacred but ineffective, we can't succumb to fear of risk fueled by doubt, resistance, and pressure. Leaders might not know how things will turn out, but when something isn't working, they must own the obligation to follow known information, make the right decisions, and execute action toward positive change.

The New Mindshift: Leading With a "Go With What Is Known" Response

In the (1984) classic *Psychology of Winning*, Waitley eloquently describes how the calm, peaceful lagoon side of the Great Barrier Reef lacks all the splendor, beauty, and life that the ocean side of the reef boasts. He reveals that the constant bombardment of the ocean on the reef creates life. It's the pressure and the struggle that offers the opportunity for growth. The willingness to confront challenges, meet issues head on, and move forward with faith is what transforms us and our schools. Again, this is counterintuitive to our self-preserving nature, but it is also the understanding and attitude that will transform schools.

The pandemic, at times, presented itself as an indomitable force, wreaking havoc on our lives, but it also unveiled incredible creativity and professionalism among educators—an implication that supports the idea that moving forward schools will succeed through acute, discriminate change. There is certainly a place for large-scale policy, such as educational standards, but as Richard Elmore observed, policy is not the solution; in fact, he advised, "become a better practitioner and get back into schools as quickly as possible. You will have a much more profound effect on the education sector working in schools" (Elmore, 2011).

This is not to downplay policies that seek to ensure that every child receives a world-class education, but those general solutions and sweeping policies create plateaus because they fail to reach the deepest corners of schooling. Impact in those areas comes from the work being done on the front lines. People in the classroom and supporting personnel are the ones who are able to make the greatest difference. This requires schools to evaluate the effectiveness of every aspect of schooling and make necessary changes based on input from the staff, research, and data. Schools need to conduct an audit to fully gauge and understand what is occurring in a school so that we know more about our actual impact and so that we look into other ways that might be better at meeting our students' needs. Audits don't inspire enthusiasm or excitement, but they do offer clarity in the current status of learning. This is the power and the necessity of our teaching and learning A.U.D.I.T. in schools.

MODEL: ACCOMPLISH, UNDERSTAND, DECIDE, INITIATE, AND TEST (A.U.D.I.T.)

The last thing we can afford to do in education is propose one more idea or solution that is packaged as an initiative but neglect to remove other initiatives to make room. Structural mechanics may be taught in some of our schools, but it is not used to determine how much the educational community can hold. Like bridges, schools are impacted by many forces and can only bear so much weight before they collapse. In schools, this is evidenced by teacher attrition, poor morale, and toxic cultures. An effective instructional A.U.D.I.T. will review all the initiatives underway, determine what needs to be eliminated, and provide insight so that leaders can go with what is known.

Our audit asks five overarching questions of the school instructional learning team, often composed of administrators, teacher leaders, and support personnel. The A.U.D.I.T. is designed to ensure that every school-wide effort is the most effective option by aligning resources and integrating systems and programs.

First Question: What Do We Want to Accomplish?

The first question is straightforward and gets right to the point. What is it that we want to *accomplish*? This question should directly tie to the Disciplined Tunnel Vision that was described in Chapter 5, along with core values and key performance indicators. Knowing the outcome is necessary for achievement and needs to be clearly understood by everyone. To ensure alignment to our Disciplined Tunnel Vision, our second question is on understanding.

Second Question: What Do We Need to Further Understand?

Too often, educational teams jump to conclusions due to their expert blind spots. The question What do we need to further *understand* to achieve our aim? prevents overlooking details or key points. Looking back on our reading focus described in Chapter 5, "asking and answering questions about unknown words in a text," the A.U.D.I.T. helps to establish the model lessons that the reading committee will develop, leveraging the most effective instructional practices.

Third Question: What Decisions Do We Need to Make?

After we have questions one and two answered, our next critical question is, What *decisions* do we need to make? This is when courage kicks in and we challenge the status quo and the untouchables that may prevent change and progress. Again, these should be aligned to our key performance indicators within a particular area but will also consider related areas like the professional learning for new staff. This is the sophistication and intersection of The Octopus Approach, Disciplined Tunnel Vision, and running an effective A.U.D.I.T. Schools are not static; plans and initiatives need to evolve as needs grow. This is why many teachers are frustrated and feel that initiatives are ineffective or irrelevant. There is little differentiation regarding the skill level of the educator. For example, if a school decides to make reading a priority then every teacher should be skilled in selecting appropriate texts, effective reading strategies, and how to provide meaningful feedback to students. However, professional development should be designed for the adult learners, their expertise, and years of experience. A new teacher should not be in the same professional development as a veteran teacher if the veteran teacher already possesses the skills to effectively preview text, implement summarization, or use questioning techniques in the classroom.

Fourth Question: What Is the Most Effective and Efficient Way to Initiate the Plan?

The next question emerges, what is the most effective and efficient way to *initiate* our path forward? This is the art of weighing each aspect of our system so that we can chart appropriate next steps. Timing is critical for success. As Mike Tyson famously said in preparation for his fight against Evander Holyfield, "Everyone has a plan until they get punched in the mouth" (Berardino, 2012). The initiation phase needs to consider all aspects of schooling identified through our systems approach.

Fifth Question: How Will We Test Our Work?

Lastly, we ask our final question: How will we *test* our work and our outcomes to determine if we are improving? Education is obsessed with inputs but often fails to accurately measure the outcomes of those inputs. We have a tendency to rely heavily on other forms of data, such as standardized tests that don't necessarily align well with the particular area that we are working to improve. The use of annual standardized assessment results perpetuates this general approach to change. Instead, schools can benefit by learning from Domino's and their persistence with ensuring that customers are satisfied. When they used customer satisfaction as the measurement for success, profit, and growth both fell into place.

These questions are represented in our model for conducting a Professional Learning Audit shown in Figure 7.1. The questions force schools to review the strategies and initiatives at every level to determine their effectiveness. The A.U.D.I.T. essentially asks why we are doing something and whether or not it is making a difference.

This process also requires everyone to dig deeper to fully understand the problem and the potential solutions. Let's consider running an A.U.D.I.T. on a common untouchable, school start times.

Model: Accomplish, Understand, Decide, Initiate, and Test

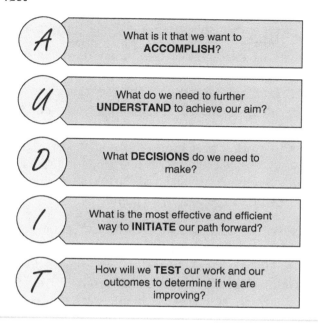

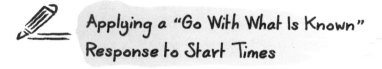

Applying a "Go With What Is Known" Response to Start Times

One of the toughest challenges in solving a problem is when the solution spirals into a host of other issues, making it difficult to determine if the risk of change is worthwhile. Sometimes one simple change, like starting school later for teens, has an incredible ripple effect, impacting many different areas. It's situations like these when leaders wish for keen insight and wisdom to make a confident decision regarding how things will play out. Unfortunately, as detailed through this chapter, many of the crossroads that leaders face aren't neat and tidy and present a great amount of uncertainty. Therefore, to reduce risk, they require a Go With What

Is Known Response, spurred by faith in the information presented.

MAKING THE CONNECTION: SCHOOL START TIMES

One of the best examples of this conundrum is pushing back middle and high school start times to 8:30 a.m. or later. On the surface it sounds simple—push back the clock and get more sleep! Yet, despite shared recommendation from both The American Medical Association and The American Academy of Pediatrics to start school later, allowing students to get the necessary "8.5 to 9.5 hours of sleep per night for optimal health and learning" (HealthDay, 2016), changing the time that the first bell rings is slow to come.

Dr. Wahlstrom, a nationally recognized expert on school start times, indicates that the evidence for starting school later is conclusive. Pushing back school start times improves students' overall well-being and health (Wahlstrom, 2014). Evidence suggests that more sleep results in improvement in areas such as attendance, tardiness, discipline, mental health, and academic performance. Researchers admit that it is hard to tell the overall significance of GPA improvement due to the variance of grading systems and other factors, but, overall, students generally do better in school when they start later (Dunster et al., 2018).

Much of this is attributed to students' improved moods and feeling less depressed. In a powerful testimony by Rick Toney, a math teacher at Solebury School, believed that only in a short amount of time, his students were less irritable, and the mornings were far less hectic. This was also felt by parents (Weller, 2017). Beyond the walls of the classroom, studies also suggest that later school times also impact better student drivers, resulting in fewer car crashes (American Academy of Sleep Medicine, 2020). With the evidence appearing overwhelmingly in favor of starting the day later, why are earlier start times still the norm? The spiral of concerns includes transportation schedules, after-school activities, athletics, and the worry that elementary students would be unsupervised after school if their older siblings had a later release time. In short, it's a logistical nightmare. This may seem trivial considering the evidence, but these justifications are what prevent us from going with what is known about start times.

This is where the mindshift must occur and recognize that many of the other efforts to improve student achievement may be negligible if we don't first concern ourselves with the health and well-being of our students. If starting school later for teens positions them to be more successful, safer, and focused, then it is a worthwhile pursuit. The limitations and restrictions of the current system cannot override the realized benefits of a later school start time.

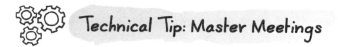 Technical Tip: Master Meetings

If there is one thing found in every school and district it's meetings. Like them or not, well run, or not, they are present in all organizations. Although often intended and designed to provide a forum for information sharing, collaboration, and decision-making, many meetings fall disastrously short of this aim. In fact, the very mention of the word, *meeting*, can elicit a negative response among many. All of us can easily recall a meeting that was not beneficial or, worse yet, a complete waste of our time. Unfortunately, poorly designed meetings are a common occurrence, but they don't have to be that way.

Planning, coordinating, and facilitating purposeful meetings is an art and one that can yield incredible results. If we don't consider one's ability to properly conduct meetings as a skill set, we are not addressing a key part of the issue. Meetings potentially house the greatest possibility for a team to accomplish its goals through the thoughts, solutions, and ideas generated. As Boudette and City (2014) write, "Great meetings are like great classrooms." Orchestrated correctly, the leader is clear on the purpose of the meeting, establishes appropriate norms, doles out individual roles, allocates a specific time, and facilitates engaging conversation, critical thinking, and problem-solving. Because structures are available that outline how to facilitate meetings effectively, using the available literature about meetings honors the theme of this chapter to apply best practices for productive meetings.

For our purpose, we are referring to recurring meetings held throughout the year in our schools and districts. These range in purpose, participants, and priorities, but, generally, these are faculty and staff meetings, planning meetings, department meetings, and so on.

It's a lack of clear purpose for a meeting that causes us to follow the same process despite the various reasons for the meetings to be held. Some meetings should be a couple of hours, while others may only need to be 15 minutes. The question is, to what degree does the meeting require participation and engagement? This provides clarity on the type and length of the meeting. It may even reveal that a meeting isn't necessary. The five different goals for meetings are to share information, create solutions, make decisions, learn and grow, and build relationships. Figure 7.2 shows the purpose for each of these goals. Every meeting should be organized to achieve one or more of these five goals.

In a visible agenda, the purpose for the meeting should be labeled next to each agenda item. For example, in Figure 7.3 there is a sample agenda from the school district calendar committee. Notice in the agenda section that each topic is listed and next to it is the purpose for that topic. The purpose for including high school start times is to create a solution. A previous agenda likely had this same item, but with the purpose of sharing information. When meeting participants are clear on the goal for the agenda topic, their dialogue can stay focused. In the sample agenda, it is not indicated that decisions will be made. The author of the agenda often knows the meeting is for brainstorming solutions, but if participants are expecting a decision to be made, they are likely to walk away

7.2 Master Meeting Planning

Goal	Purpose
Share information	Disseminate and discuss pertinent updates and news that needs some degree of explanation that is too large or complex for an email.
Create solutions	Determine possible solutions to issues that do not have an easy answer or clear decision that requires input from a few sources.
Make decisions	Determinations that need to be made on a particular issue.
Learn and grow	Activities designed to develop the overall capacity of the group.
Build relationships	Activities designed to help individuals get to know one another to maximize the strengths of the group.

Source: Adapted from the works of Boudette and City (2014), Chang and Merta (2004), and Lencioni (1999).

thinking the meeting was a waste of time. By identifying the purpose of the agenda item, the group easily grasps their role and expectations. This is what ineffective meetings lack, a clear focus on meaningful and relevant issues that require challenging discourse (Lencioni, 2004). Meetings don't have to be sit and get, mundane, and boring; all these experiences are avoidable. Lastly, meetings should have outcomes identified and detailed with a clear understanding of "who will do what by when" (Hanson & Hanson, 2005). Designating a place on the agenda to document next steps, person responsible, and a due date will secure which actions will be taken after the meeting and by whom.

Effective meetings hold the potential to radically change the course of any school in a positive direction. They serve as hubs for the most difficult but necessary conversations. Meetings serve as the primary space to wrestle with challenging issues and ideas, review the latest research, "rumble" with ideas,

7.3 Sample Meeting Agenda

School Calendar Committee Meeting		Date:	
Participants	**Roles**	**Purpose Key**	
1. 2. 3. 4. 5. 6. 7.	Facilitator: Notetaker: Timekeeper: Alternate:	Share Information (SI) Create Solutions (CS) Make Decisions (MD) Learn and Grow (LG) Build Relationships (BR)	
Agenda Item	**Time Allocated**	**Purpose**	
Share good news Parent survey review Corwin Connect article High school start times Summary and closure	2 minutes 7 minutes 8 minutes 20 minutes 3 minutes	(BR) (SI) (LG) (CS) (SI)	
Notes:			
Next Steps	**Person Responsible**	**Due Date**	
• • • •			

and come to the best solutions. Meetings engage a community of thinkers who need to make sound, research-based decisions that will yield the greatest result. Conducted well, they become the staple of collaboration within every school and district. This technical tip, like each one presented in previous chapters, stems from available information that can and should be put into practice.

Reflection Questions

1. How does a Go With What Is Known Response align with how decisions are made in your school?

2. What are some untouchables in your school that could benefit from a Go With What Is Known Response? How might you initiate this mindshift?

3. What information do you know, or suspect, is available about a persistent problem in your school that isn't being applied? Where/How can you find out what is known?

4. Think about a meeting you will be leading in the future. How can the technical tip to Master Meetings help you get the most out of the team's time?

CONCLUSION
LEADING TO MAXIMIZE DISRUPTION

When a perpetual problem qualifies as important, urgent, and persistent, we assert that it reaches a new level—a status that requires us to categorize it as an educational crisis. When a crisis hits, our thinking and leading shifts. Making it through the crisis, stabilizing the situation, and working to reach a productive outcome amid an awful situation becomes everyone's priority. There is an understanding among those affiliated with the crisis that something must be done—even if the action isn't guaranteed to be the ultimate solution. Sitting idly by and doing nothing is not on the table. Even minor action is not an option. Being in crisis mode puts everyone in a different frame of behaving and thinking. It triggers all-hands-on-deck, softens rigid parameters, and instigates divergent thinking. Priorities are clear and everyone is laser-focused. This ethos has proven to overcome barriers previously thought to be insurmountable.

It Took a Pandemic

What happened in education during the COVID-19 pandemic is an example of the extraordinary feats that emerge from chaos. Ask any educator what their first reaction was to the March 2020 announcement that schools would be shut down. There was an immediate denial that teaching and learning could occur if the doors to every school were closed for an extended period of time. Initially, the disbelief was so strong that many schools didn't even make an effort to shift to remote learning or plan for long-term closures. Why? Too many obstacles were in place. In other words, flawed thinking. For various stretches of time, we denied that there was any way to remove these barriers. We were immobilized.

As the fears became a terrifying reality, schools started planning for a situation that not only no one had predicted but that no one had even fathomed. Whether we intended to or not, we were thrown into a beginner's mind because there wasn't a soul around who even pretended to know what to do. As the unknowns persisted, educators began to reckon with the gravity of the situation and started to explore options. From the chaos that ensued, ideas like conducting the teaching and learning from home emerged. When people responded with "yeah, but," they were immediately met with "Yes, And." As educators accepted the facts, the enormity of the crisis was faced, and piece-by-piece, we got to work.

It wasn't easy. Obstacles like "Yeah, but not every student has a computer at home" were countered with "Yes, and we will need to establish a way to disperse Chromebooks to them." Or "Yeah, but students don't have internet access to use the learning management system" was met with "Yes, and we need to ensure that they have connectivity." The goal to educate students at home was clear, and no other possibilities existed. It forced schools to gather what they knew and move to the battleground to access every available resource to provide students with paths to education and a much-needed network of support.

Providing resources and connection for students to learn at home was just one of the hurdles. Educators questioned how many of our students would eat good meals, and who would talk to the student who had been experiencing depression, and, worse yet, what will we do with those who live in a toxic home environment? As educators worked relentlessly to address each arm of the problem within the system, one mission was consistent—provide services, support, and learning to the students we had the responsibility to educate. This sharp focus on the purpose was shared with the community, families, and the entire education system. We acknowledge that there were political differences, but even with opposing views on *how* it would be done, there was no pushback on *if* it should be done. We acknowledged the crisis, and solutions developed more quickly than ever before—not just for problems that the pandemic caused but even for ones that we seemingly couldn't solve before the pandemic hit. During the pandemic, front-line educators applied the seven mindshifts that we have shared in this book. Let's visit some of their examples as you reflect on accomplishments you achieved from this crisis and what that means for the future.

If leaders, like those represented in our imaginary Elmore School District, can find solutions in the midst of turmoil and uncertainty, imagine what can be done when a crisis mindset is intentionally engaged.

THE ELMORE SCHOOL DISTRICTS OF THE WORLD

To illustrate some examples of how the seven mindshifts have been applied by leaders, we combined the stories from multiple schools and created a new fictitious school district that we named Elmore School District. The stories shared about Elmore Schools are inspired by actual schools which shifted their thinking and experienced various levels of success during the pandemic of 2020 and beyond. There are countless schools which stepped up and did what needed to be done, not knowing the mountainous feats they would accomplish. Perhaps they even surprised themselves. If leaders, like those represented in our imaginary Elmore School District, can find solutions in the midst of turmoil and uncertainty, imagine what can be done when a crisis mindset is intentionally engaged.

Elmore School District: Leading With a Crisis Mindset

Every year, Elmore Schools struggled with mass absences when flu season hit. It was such an issue that the benchmark assessment calendar intentionally avoided February when sicknesses were at their peak. While this was indeed an important, urgent, and persistent problem, it was accepted as reality and the school planned around it. In Fall of 2020, when teams of educators planned for students to return to school buildings part time, there was a heightened focus on health and safety. Staggered lunch schedules were created so fewer students were in the lunchroom, and hand washing stations were installed all over the school. The custodial staff was trained to disinfect classrooms every night. Cohorts of students stayed together throughout the day to limit their exposure to multiple peers.

While there was some disagreement in the community about a few of these new practices and policies, the results of Elmore's efforts allowed students to return to classrooms and an unintended consequence of their diligent safety measures emerged. Attendance during flu season was stable. The increase in absences that they typically saw every February was not present in February 2021. As social distancing restrictions loosened, habits like hand washing, teaching students to cough into their elbow, and sanitizing practices remained. It took a pandemic for the flu season crisis to be resolved, and we are happy to report that, in February 2022, attendance was stable for a second consecutive year. Elmore's students and staff had fewer cases of cold or flu than any other time in history.

Elmore School District: Leading With a Battleground Mentality

It wasn't long after the 2020 school shutdowns that Elmore's school leaders started to worry about the many students who relied on school for two of their three meals per day. Food service, transportation, and administration initiated a Battleground Mentality to let nothing stand in the way of providing healthy meals for kids. With relentless determination, they figured out a way to offer daily curbside pick-up for families to drive up and collect food. They experimented with locations and times to find the most convenient options for their community.

Soon, they realized the meal delivery service was going to continue for an extended time, which meant that their agility was put to the test. Instead of daily pick-ups, they flexed to providing a week's worth of meals at a time. When they learned that some families were still not able to take advantage of the school-provided meals, they sought ways to have bus drivers deliver boxes of food to homes, ready to be prepped, and enjoyed by the Elmore School District's families. In a matter of months, the team had a system down pat that not only provided breakfast and lunch to every Elmore family, but they partnered with a local business to offer dinner for all families who qualified for free/reduced lunch. This community service of providing a third meal for families who need it continues today.

Elmore School District: Leading With a Beginner's Mind

Prior to the pandemic, in Fall 2019, the Elmore counseling team rallied together to advocate their department be doubled in staff. Their team was unable to meet the rapidly growing mental health needs of their students. Social and emotional supports were needed at every level and the counselors knew that pulling students from class was only making matters worse. Elmore is a district with a tradition of high achievement and the staff prided themselves with its focus on academics.

Months later, teachers shared their observations about how students' mental health struggles were impeding their ability to learn at the same rate as "normal." As the counselors brainstormed ways to support teachers and students, they put themselves in the position of the teachers. Their ability to see the problem from a Beginner's Mind led them to create multiple strategies to emphasize the social and emotional learning (SEL) of students. They developed a bank of SEL activities that fostered student/teacher connections. A schedule was created to provide small groups and even one-on-one time with students. Teachers were provided basic coping skills they could share with students, and the majority of students were getting the attention they required for their SEL needs. Now, Elmore's teachers incorporate SEL practices in their daily routines to continue to focus on the whole child.

Elmore School District: Leading With an Octopus Approach

Everything during the pandemic required an Octopus Approach for Elmore. The domino effect of one thing impacting another

(Continued)

was amazing. On a grand scale, the problem was that students and teachers were not in the school building so connecting with them was a major issue. It's one thing to broadcast messages, send emails, or even do a video to communicate, but it is another to make sure people are receiving and listening to what is being shared. As the tentacles emerged to define the complexity of that giant problem, mini octopuses emerged, each with its own set of arms. For example, the first few weeks of the pandemic were filled with uncertainty, disbelief, and angst. We've referenced the need for schools to mobilize fast from cleaning and disinfecting schools to providing meals, but all of this required intense and massive communication.

Elmore quickly realized that in the absence of information people were creating their own information. This was amassing a different level of chaos. As a result, they used the Octopus Approach by identifying every school division, school leadership team, community group, the state department of education, any other agency they could think of, and other school districts. They then built a new communication flow that originated with the Superintendent because she was receiving the communications first from many of the other agencies. They developed a system to ensure that every group received the details needed in a regular cadence with when they needed to know about something new or a change that was made. Knowing that people's lives were completely upended, and many families were fighting the virus, the teams circled back to key topics and information to make sure everyone was on the same page as much as possible. We're happy to say that communication in the Elmore School District is forever changed for the better.

Elmore School District: Leading With a Disciplined Tunnel Vision

When the pandemic hit, Elmore Schools needed new timetables for how students experienced school from home. Traditional rigid thinking about bell schedules and seat time was out-the-window. Accumulating time "in school" was no longer on the table in any form, which meant that leaders needed to come up with a new vision for how schooling would occur in both synchronized and asynchronous formats. At every level, school would be different and there was no blueprint to follow.

Mr. Gander, the technology coordinator, worked closely with Mrs. Ware, one of the school's principals. Together, they systematically identified their new vision for what teaching and learning would look like and committed to core values of educating the whole child and delivering quality instruction.

The duo led a team of educators who put together schedules that included scheduled and unscheduled online learning. With a significantly higher amount of asynchronous learning planned in the students' week, new platforms and tools to support independent learning were initially explored. Then, as teachers found success with a specific program, like Google Classroom or an app such as Nearpod, they were swiftly shared as models for other teachers to replicate. As expected, new problems like grading and tracking evidence surfaced. When they did, the team added the concerns to the list, confirmed their priorities, and disciplined themselves to give each dilemma their full attention.

Quickly and consistently, piece-by-piece, everyone grew stronger at the new methods of instruction that required Elmore staff to think about time and resources differently than they had in the past. When the fully remote model shifted to a hybrid schedule, they went through the same process and again when everyone returned to school. Now, whenever a big change needs to be made, they follow the similar step-by-step pattern by establishing a clear vision and working toward models of implementation.

Elmore School District: Leading With a "Yes, And" Attitude

In March 2020, leadership teams in Elmore Schools struggled with how to provide instruction to students when schools were closed. "Yeah, but" thinking provided barriers to moving to online learning. Instructional teams voiced that "we are simply not ready to move to full online learning." Even with the solution to distribute Chromebooks to families and after resolving all of the issues associated with distribution, internet access surfaced as the next "yeah, but." People thought, "What good is a computer if they don't have the internet?" These types of thoughts permeated meetings, but with the right mindshift, the team's persistent use of a "Yes, And" attitude led to the distribution of additional technology support, providing hotspots for families who needed them.

(Continued)

This started with identifying who had the internet and who needed the internet. In the meantime, some parts of the district simply weren't equipped with necessary infrastructure in the community to support the internet, regardless of hotspots. Once the Elmore team had a very good understanding of the needs, they worked with different companies that could provide internet connectivity. However, the "Yes, And" attitude was never satisfied with just the right tools. For those who had significantly limited access, paper materials were created. Instructional services shifted into overdrive to work with building-based teams to create and get the work to students. For those with devices, and now connectivity, Elmore devised teams to train teachers on proven online learning practices, the most effective and the simplest to implement. For students, the same thing occurred with expectations around what online learning sounded like and looked like from home. Now that these structures are in place, an online component of teaching and learning is still used by teachers and students. A student's learning location will never be a barrier again.

Elmore School District: Leading With a "Go With What Is Known" Response

It wasn't long before Dr. Richards, the Special Population Coordinator in Elmore Schools, recognized that students who required specific services were not receiving them when the school was remote. In order to make changes to the new structures, IEPs and 504 Plans had to be revisited. Another octopus arm was that caregivers were an important and necessary part of the decision-making process.

Rather than discluding families, Dr. Richards was determined to Go With What Is Known and find a way to allow key stakeholders to be present to make decisions about programming for students. Special meetings moved to an online setting. This practice of offering remote attendance is now common for Elmore, even though the school is open and team members can participate face-to-face. Making meetings more accessible to caretakers has not only continued but also many families and other agencies prefer it as an option to not have to drive to the school for every meeting.

The narrative descriptions of Elmore School District illustrate the significant strides that real schools made throughout the crisis of the pandemic. The tangled interconnectedness made decisions complex and intricate, but the pandemic revealed how schools, and the people within them, are capable of astounding changes. It is a point of pride and inspiration that educators rallied with true clarity and purpose, and in many ways, came out better than they were before. If nothing else, educators everywhere had evidence of what could be accomplished when they used the crisis to shift their thinking in novel ways. The looming question of "how are we going to educate and support our children?" filled everyone's hearts, and they made a determination to do whatever it takes. They made a mindshift and applied a crisis mindset.

Systemic Change for a Better Tomorrow

As optimists and believers in the power of schooling, looking back on this historical event, we saw how some schools took the opportunity to maximize the disruption and create better learning environments for students. Instructionally, they took what worked with blended learning and created varying options for student seat time. Now that nearly everyone knows how to engage in video conferencing, our ability to communicate with speed and efficiency has improved, creating the boundaryless organization that helps decentralizing schools and give others a voice. Think of our focus on health by asking any kindergarten teacher who spends most of the winter months wiping noses and teaching students to cough into their elbows. Protocols for disinfecting didn't emerge because of COVID-19, but our awareness of healthy habits has been acutely heightened—to the benefit of the health of students and staff. Conditions for learning like engagement, feedback, collaboration, grading, homework, and more are being revisited from a more critical perspective. The schools that have leveraged the pandemic to improve their systems are the ones that have made mindshifts and embraced a crisis mindset. Their systems changed. Their tomorrow is different from yesterday.

The polar opposite is sadly true as well. Schools that responded to the crisis with flawed thinking seemed to be waiting until the pandemic ended so that they could revert back to what they knew as "normal." We shake our heads at the lost potential. It's akin to having emergency triple bypass surgery, only to leave the hospital with a cigarette in your hand while eating a cheeseburger, heavily salted fries, and a warm apple pie. Whether we like it or not, the pandemic provided a time for a do-over. If we don't reflect on the crisis and learn from the conditions we faced, we will lose the opportunity to improve our schools on a systemic level.

If we can move mountains to educate students through a pandemic, rally the community to offer support and services, and suspend rigid ideas of what learning looks like, then surely we can come together with the same ruthless diligence to overcome other issues.

Although our reflection of the opportunities that presented themselves during COVID-19 is what brought this book's concept to light, it's the lack of a dogged effort and continuous action until problems are solved that demand attention. If we can move mountains to educate students through a pandemic, rally the community to offer support and services, and suspend rigid ideas of what learning looks like, then surely we can come together with the same ruthless diligence to overcome other issues such as teaching students with interrupted formal education, repairing harm caused by behavior, raising third-grade reading scores, providing equity for students in historically marginalized groups, employing and maintaining quality teachers, and the list goes on. These problems are not going away. They have been on the back burner for too long. They are persistent, urgent, and important. These are the crises we face in education, and with the conscious choice to think about these old problems in new and intentional ways, we can solve them.

Reflection Questions

1. Think about a crisis your school is facing. What potential do you see to harness the disruption to motivate your team toward an ultimate solution?

2. Which of the seven mindshifts would be easiest for you to embrace tomorrow? Which is the most challenging? Why?

3. In what three ways might Leading With a Crisis Mindset (embracing all seven mindshifts) change your leadership style?

4. List three perennial problems in your school that need a crisis mindset to solve. What next steps will you take this month to tackle these crises?

REFERENCES

Ackoff, R. (2003). *Ackoff seminars* [Video]. https://www.youtube.com/watch?v=a0ooqJ-pOH4&t=33s

Alsop, T. (2022, January 10). *Tablets, laptops & PCS sales forecast 2025*. Statista. Retrieved March 26, 2022, from https://www.statista.com/statistics/272595/global-shipments-forecast-for-tablets-laptops-and-desktop-pcs/

American Academy of Sleep Medicine. (2020, February 18). *Later school start times reduce car crashes, improve teen safety*. Science Daily. Retrieved from https://www.sciencedaily.com/releases/2020/02/200218125312.htm

American Oceans. (n.d.). *How many suction cups does an Octopus have?* Retrieved from https://www.americanoceans.org/facts/how-many-suction-cups-giant-pacific-octopus/

Ancona, D., Malone, T., Orlikowski, W., & Senge, P. (2007). In praise of the incomplete leader. *Harvard Business Review*. Retrieved January 7, 2018, from https://hbr.org/2007/02/in-praise-of-the-incomplete-leader

Argyris, C. (1992). *On organizational learning*. Malden, MA: Blackwell Publishers.

Artelta, M. (Director). (2021). *Yes Day* [Film]. Grey Matter Productions Entertainment 360.

Ashkenas, R. (2015, September 09). Jack Welch's approach to breaking down silos still works. *Harvard Business Review*. Retrieved December 19, 2021, from https://hbr.org/2015/09/jack-welchs-approach-to-breaking-down-silos-still-works

Automobile Topics of Interest; Many Amateurs are Building Machines from Purchased Parts—How the Industry Resembles the Cycling Fad—Gen Stone Working for Steel Roads for the New Vehicles. (1902, July 13). *TimesMachine*. Retrieved March 31, 2022, from https://timesmachine.nytimes.com/timesmachine/1902/07/13/101276726.html?pageNumber=12

Azriel, O., & Bar-Haim, Y. (2020). Attention bias. In J. S. Abramowitz & S. M. Blakey (Eds.), *Clinical handbook of fear and anxiety: Maintenance processes and treatment mechanisms* (pp. 203-218). American Psychological Association. 10.1037/0000150-012

Baldoni, J. (2016). *Temperament: What it takes to lead.* SmartBrief. Retrieved on January 7, 2018, from https://www.smartbrief.com/original/2016/11/temperament-what-it-takes-lead

Bartoletti, J., & Connelly, G. (2013). *Leadership matters: What the research says about the importance of principal leadership.* NASSP & NAESP.

Bazerman, M. (2014). *The power of noticing: What the best leaders see.* New York, NY: Simon & Schuster Paperbacks.

Berardino, M. (2012). *Mike Tyson explains one of his most famous quotes.* South Florida, Sun Sentinal. Retrieved from https://www.sun-sentinel.com/sports/fl-xpm-2012-11-09-sfl-mike-tyson-explains-one-of-his-most-famous-quotes-20121109-story.html

Berger, W. (2019). *A more beautiful question: The power of inquiry to spark breakthrough ideas.* Vancouver, BC: Langara College.

Bernhardt, V. (1998). *Data analysis: For comprehensive schoolwide improvement.* Larchmont, NY: Eye On Education.

Bezodis, N., Willwacher, S., & Salo, A. (2019). *The biomechanics of the track and field sprint start: A narrative review.* Retrieved from https://www.ncbi.nlm.nih.gov/pmc/articles/PMC6684547/

Bostock, B. (2020, March 2). Jack Welch, former general electric CEO who influenced generations of business leaders, has died at 84. *Inc.com.* Retrieved December 19, 2021, from https://www.inc.com/business-insider/jack-welch-ceo-general-electric-dead-died.html

Boudette, K. P., & City, E. A. (2014). *Meeting wise: Making the most of collaborative time for educators.* Cambridge, MA: Harvard Education Press.

Boyes, A. (2018, September 20). 4 ways busy people sabotage themselves. *Harvard Business Review.* Retrieved from https://hbr.org/2018/09/4-ways-busy-people-sabotage-themselves

Bradberry, T. (2016, September 9). How complaining rewires your brain for negativity. *Entrepreneur.* Retrieved December 15, 2021, from https://www.entrepreneur.com/article/281734

Brinkerhoff, E. H., & Roehrig, A. D. (2014). *No more sharpening pencils during work time and other time wasters.* Portsmouth, NH: Heinemann.

Brooks, N. (2020, December 21). *What causes tunnel vision, and what are the treatments.* Medical News Today. Retrieved from https://www.medicalnewstoday.com/articles/tunnel-vision

Brown, L. (2007). *Up thoughts for down times: Encouraging words for getting through life.* ELEVATE.

Brown, B. (2015). *Daring greatly: How the courage to be vulnerable transforms the way we live, love, parent, and lead.* New York, NY: Penguin Random House.

Brown, B. (2019). *Let's rumble.* Retrieved on December 30, 2021, from https://brenebrown.com/articles/2019/05/01/lets-rumble/

Capek Tingley, S. (n.d.). *Should students have homework?* Western Governors University. Retrieved from https://www.wgu.edu/heyteach/article/should-students-have-homework1808.html

Carver-Thomas, D., & Darling-Hammond, L. (2017). *Teacher turnover: Why it matters and what we can do about it.* Palo Alto, CA: Learning Policy Institute.

Cepelewicz, J. (2019). To pay attention, the brain uses filters, not a spotlight. *Quanta Magazine.* Retrieved from https://www.quantamagazine.org/to-pay-attention-the-brain-uses-filters-not-a-spotlight-20190924/

Chamorro-Premuzic, T., & Bersin, J. (2018, July 12). 4 ways to create a learning culture on your team. *Harvard Business Review.* Retrieved from https://hbr.org/2018/07/4-ways-to-create-a-learning-culture-on-your-team

Chang, R. Y., & Merta, J. P. (1999). *Meetings that work in education.* Irvine, CA: Richard Chang Associates.

Chow, V. (2016). *Shanghai fools: An uplifting, heart-warming romantic comedy (Master shanghai book 2)* (1st ed., Vol. 2). Scotts Valley, CA: CreateSpace Independent Publishing Platform.

Clark, R., Feldon, D., Van Merrienboer, J. J. G., Yates, K., & Early, S. (2008). Cognitive task analysis. In *Handbook of research on educational communications and technology* (pp. 577-593). New York, NY: Macmillan/Gale.

Clear, J. (2018, June 12). Shoshin: A remarkable zen concept used to let go of old assumptions. *James Clear.* Retrieved from https://jamesclear.com/shoshin

Cobb, F., & Krownapple, J. (2019). *Belonging through a culture of dignity: The keys to successful equity implementation* (p. 180). San Diego, CA: Mimi and Todd Press.

Collins, J. (2022). *Five stages of decline.* Retrieved from https://www.jimcollins.com/concepts/five-stages-of-decline.html

Covey, S. (1989). *Seven habits of highly effective people: Restoring the character ethic.* Vol. 1. New York, NY: Simon & Schuster.

Dalio, R. (2017). *Principles: Life and work.* New York, NY: Simon & Schuster.

De Bono, E. (2016). *Six Thinking Hats.* Penguin UK.

Decker, P., & Mitchell, J. (2016, December 15). Tunnel vision—It's drawbacks and how to stay clear of it. *Manage Magazine.* Retrieved from https://managemagazine.com/article-bank/self-handicapping-leadership/tunnel-vision-its-drawbacks-and-how-to-stay-clear-of-it/

Duckworth, A. (2016). *Grit: The power of passion and perseverance.* Scribner/Simon & Schuster.

Duncan, A. (2019). *How schools work: An inside account of failure and success from one of the nation's longest-serving secretaries of education.* New York, NY: Simon & Schuster.

Dunster, G. P., de la Iglesia, L., Ben-Hamo, M., Nave, C., Fleischer, J. G., Panda, S., & de la Iglesia, H. O. (2018). Sleepmore in Seattle: Later school start times are associated with more sleep and better performance in high school students. *Science Advances.* 4(2). Retrieved from https://www.science.org/doi/10.1126/sciadv.aau6200

Dweck, C. S. (2007). *Mindset: The new psychology of success.* New York, NY: Penguin Random House, LLC.

Dweck, C. (2015). Carol Dweck revisits the 'growth mindset'. *Education Week.* Retrieved from http://www.edweek.org/ew/articles/2015/09/23/carol-dweck-revisits-the-growth-mindset.html?cmp=cpc-goog-ew-growth+mindset&ccid=growth+mindset&ccag=growth+mindset&cckw=%2Bgrowth%20%2Bmindset&cccv=content+ad&gclid=Cj0KEQiAnvfDBRCXrabLl6-6t-0BEiQAW4SRUM7nekFnoTxc675qBMSJycFgwERohguZWVmNDcSUg5gaAk3I8P8HAQ

Economy, P. (2015). Mark Cuban: 19 Inspiring power quotes for success. *Inc.com.* Retrieved from https://www.inc.com/business-insider/17-best-mark-cuban-quotes.html

Edwards, P. (2015, June 29). 7 world-changing inventions people thought were dumb fads. *Vox.* Retrieved from https://www.vox.com/2015/2/9/8004661/fads-inventions-changed-world

Elmore, R. (2002). Hard questions about practice. *Education Leadership,* 59(8), 22-25. ASCD.

Elmore, R. (June 14, 2011). *"I used to think ... and now I think..."* Retrieved from https://www.hepg.org/blog/i-used-to-think-and-now-i-think-%E2%80%9D

Feldman, J. (2019). *Grading for equity: What it is, why it matters, and how it can transform schools and classrooms.* Thousand Oaks, CA: Corwin.

Fisher, R., & Ury, W. (2011). *Getting to yes: Negotiating agreement without giving in* (3rd ed). New York, NY: Penguin Books.

Flory, E. (2007). *Giant pacific octopus.* Retrieved from https://sea grant.oregonstate.edu/sites/seagrant.oregonstate.edu/files/sgpubs/onlinepubs/g07002.pdf

Fromm, A., & Kander, D. (2018). *The curiosity muscle: A story of how four simple questions uncover powerful insights and exponential growth.* TrueFolio Publishing.

Fullan, M., & Quinn, J. (2016). *Coherence: The right drivers in action for schools, districts, and systems.* Thousand Oaks, CA: Corwin.

Gallup. (2014). *State of American schools.*

Gallup. (2017, March 27). *Your focus talent: Beneficial tunnel vision.* Cliftonstrengths. Retrieved from https://www.gallup.com/clifton strengths/en/250322/focus-talent-beneficial-tunnel-vision.aspx

Garvin, D. (1993). Building a learning organization. *Harvard Business Review,* Retrieved from https://hbr.org/1993/07/building-a-learning-organization

George, M., Rowlands, D., Price, M., & Maxey, J. (2004). *The lean six sigma pocket toolbook: A quick reference guide to 100 tools for improving quality and speed by Michael L. George.* McGraw-Hill Education.

Goman, C. K. (2011). Forbes. *The art and science of mirroring.* Retrieved from https://www.forbes.com/sites/carolkinseygoman/2011/05/31/the-art-and-science-of-mirroring/?sh=3d313c621318

Gopnik, A. (2011). *The philosophical baby: What children's minds tell us about truth, love & the meaning of life.* London; Vintage Digital.

Grant, A. (2021). *Think again: The power of knowing what you don't know.* New York, NY: Viking.

Grifhorst, J., Lessway, J., & Zamborowski, M. (2012). Alternative to round robin reading. *Michigan Reading Journal,* 44(2). Retrieved from https://scholarworks.gvsu.edu/cgi/viewcontent.cgi?article=1181&context=mrj

Guskey, T., & Brookhart, S. (2019). *What we know about grading: What works, what doesn't, and what's next.* Alexandria, VA: ASCD.

Haden, J. (2021). *10 years ago, "cardboard" pizza almost killed Domino's. Then, Domino's did something brilliant.* Inc.com. Retrieved from https://www.inc.com/jeff-haden/10-years-ago-

cardboard-pizza-almost-killed-dominos-then-dominos-did-some
thing-brilliant.html

Hanson, T., & Hanson, B. Z. (2005). *Who will do what by when. How to improve performance, accountability and trust with integrity.* Power Publications.

Harris, D. (n.d.) *Work-out: The most powerful process improvement tool.* Retrieved from https://www.isixsigma.com/new-to-six-sigma/roles-responsibilities/work-out-most-powerful-process-improvement-tool/

Harris, P. L. (2012). *Trusting what you're told: How children learn from others.* Harvard University Press.

Hartmans, A. (August 23, 2018). *These 18 incredible products didn't exist 10 years ago.* Business Insider Nederland. Retrieved March 31, 2022, from https://www.businessinsider.nl/18-tech-products-that-didnt-exist-10-years-ago-2017-7?international=true&r=US

Hattie, J. (2009). *Visible learning: A synthesis of over 800 meta-analyses relating to achievement.* London: Routledge.

Hattie, J. (2016). *Assessment - feedback about impact.* https://www.myedresource.com/2016/01/19/assessment-feedback-about-impact/#:~:text=By%20using%20formative%20assessment%20as,diagnose%2C%20intervene%2C%20and%20evaluate

Hattie, J. (2021, August). *Cognitive task analysis.* Corwin Visible Learning plus. Retrieved January 16, 2022, from https://www.visiblelearningmetax.com/influences/view/cognitive_task_analysis

HealthDay. (2016). *Later school start times means better-rested kids-study.* Retrieved from https://consumer.healthday.com/b-4-15-later-school-start-times-mean-better-rested-kids-study-2652238011.html

Hughes, J. N., West, S. G., Kim, H., & Bauer, S. S. (2018). Effect of early grade retention on school completion: A prospective study. *Journal of Educational Psychology,* 110(7), 974–991. doi:10.1037/edu0000243

Janacsek, K., Fiser, J., & Nemeth, D. (2012). The best time to acquire new skills: Age-related differences in implicit sequence learning across the human lifespan. *Developmental Science,* 15(4), 496-505. doi:10.1111/j.1467-7687.2012.01150.x

Jensen, A., & Barron, J. (2014, November/December). Midterm and first-exam grades predict final grades in biology courses. *Journal of College Science Teaching,* 44, 82–89.

Jones, J., Thomas-EL, S., & Vari, T. (2020). *Building a winning team: The power of a magnetic reputation and the need to recruit top talent in every school.* New York, NY: Rowman & Littlefield.

Jones, J., & Vari, T. (Hosts). (2017, November 19). #onethingseries: The power of positivity w/@JonGordon11. [Audio podcast episode]. TheOnethingSeries. *TheSchoolHouse302*. Retreived from https://theschoolhouse302.com/2017/11/19/onethingseries-the-power-of-positivity-w-jongordon11/

Kafele, B. (2021). *The equity & social justice education: Critical questions for improving opportunities and outcomes for Black students.* Alexandria, VA: ASCD.

Kirsch, V., Bildner, J., & Walker, J. (2016). Why social ventures need systems thinking. *Harvard Business Review.* Retrieved December 19, 2021, from https://hbr.org/2016/07/why-social-ventures-need-systems-thinking

Kotter, J. (1996). *Leading change.* Boston, MA: Harvard Business Review Press.

Lee, S. W. (2018). Pulling back the curtain: Revealing the cumulative importance of high-performing, highly qualified teachers on students' educational outcome. *Educational Evaluation and Policy Analysis, 40*(3), 359-381. doi:10.3102/0162373718769379

Lencioni, P. (2004). *Death by meeting: A leadership fable.* San Francisco, CA: Jossy Bass.

Lencioni, P. (2012). *The advantage: Why organizational health trumps everything else in business.* San Francisco, CA: Jossey-Bass.

Leonard, K., & Yorton, T. (2015). *Yes, and: How improvisation reverses "no, but" thinking and improves creativity and collaboration—lessons from the second city.* Harper Business.

Lieber, R. (2016, July 1). Why your financial life feels like a whac-a-mole. *The New York Times.* Retrieved from https://www.nytimes.com/2016/07/02/your-money/why-your-financial-life-feels-like-whac-a-mole.html

Luchins, A. (1942). Mechanization in problem solving: The effect of Einstellung. *Psychological Monographs, 54*(6), i-95.

Luchins, A. S., & Luchins, E. H. (1959). *Rigidity of behavior: A variational approach to the effect of Einstellung.* University of Oregon Books. ISBN 9780871140074. OCLC 14598941.

Ma, L. (2014). Psychology Today. *Power of Humor in Ideation and Creativity.* Retrieved from https://www.psychologytoday.com/us/blog/the-tao-innovation/201406/the-power-humor-in-ideation-and-creativity

Ma, L. (2015). The power of humor in ideation and creativity. *Psychology Today.* Retrieved from https://www.psychologytoday.com/us/blog/the-tao-innovation/201406/the-power-humor-in-ideation-and-creativity

Mad About Science. (2018, May 6). *Spaghetti and marshmallow tower*. Retrieved from https://www.madaboutscience.com.au/shop/science-extra/post/spaghetti-and-marshmallow-tower

Maltz, M. (1976). *Psycho-cybernetics: A new way to get more living out of life*. North Hollywood, CA: Wilshire Book.

Minkel, J. (2015). *Why I prefer pre-teaching to remediation for struggling students*. Published Online: Retrieved May 18, 2015. https://www.edweek.org/teaching-learning/opinion-why-i-prefer-pre-teaching-to-remediation-for-struggling-students/2015/05

Montague, S. (2014, August 20). *John Hattie on BBC radio 4: "Homework in primary schools has effect of zero"* [a radio interview with professor and author John Hattie]. Retrieved from https://visible-learning.org/2014/09/john-hattie-interview-bbc-radio-4/

Maynard, N., & Weinstein, B. (2019). Hacking School Discipline: 9 Ways to Create a Culture of Empathy and Responsibility Using Restorative Justice (Hack Learning Series). Times 10 Publications.

Nag, U. (2020). *Usain Bolt's records: Best strikes from the lightning bolt*. Retrieved from https://olympics.com/en/featured-news/usain-bolt-record-world-champion-athlete-fastest-man-olympics-sprinter-100m-200m

Nathan, M. J., Koedinger, K. R., & Alibali, M. W. (n.d.). *Expert blind spot: When content knowledge and pedagogical knowledge collide*. Retrieved from https://www.colorado.edu/ics/sites/default/files/attached-files/00-05.pdf

National Center for Homeless Education. (2021). *Student homelessness in America: School years 2017-18 to 2019-20*. Retrieved from https://nche.ed.gov/wp-content/uploads/2021/12/Student-Homelessness-in-America-2021.pdf

National Center for Homeless Education. (n.d.). *The McKinney-Vento homeless assistance act*. Retrieved from https://nche.ed.gov/legislation/mckinney-vento/

National Governors Association Center for Best Practices, & Council of Chief State School Officers. (2010). *Common core state standards for mathematics: Standards for mathematical practice*. Retrieved from http://www.corestandards.org/Math/Practice/

National Wildlife Federation. (n.d.). *Octopuses*. Retrieved from https://www.nwf.org/Educational-Resources/Wildlife-Guide/Invertebrates/Octopuses

National society of high school scholars. (2021, May 11). Retrieved from https://www.nshss.org/blog/equity-vs-equality-in-educa tion-why-both-are-essential-in-today-s-classrooms/#:~:text= Equality%20in%20education%20is%20necessary,need%20extra% 20help%20and%20attention

Nelson, H. G., & Stolterman, E. (2003). *The design way: Intentional change in an unpredictable world.* Englewood Cliffs, NJ: Educational Technology Publications.

Nuwer, R. (2013). Severed octopus' arms have a mind of their own. *Smithsonian Magazine.* Retrieved from https://www.smithso nianmag.com/smart-news/severed-octopus-arms-have-a-mind- of-their-own-2403303/

NYESD. (n.d.). *Students with interrupted/inconsistent formal edu- cation (SIFE).* Retrieved from http://www.nysed.gov/common/ nysed/files/programs/bilingual-ed/sife_q_a_9_20_16.pdf

Oceana. (n.d.). *Giant pacific octopus.* Retrieved from https:// oceana.org/marine-life/giant-pacific-octopus/?gclid=CjwKCAiA78 aNBhAlEiwA7B76p5cGnAu3tfTFGwRRbap-zOpEwlIVKqd10B5aq0y9Nrs zZsqLlVpbuhoC9ZoQAvD_BwE&utm_campaign=engage&utm_ content=ga2&utm_source=google&utm_medium=cpc

Randolph, M. (2019). *That will never work: The birth of Netflix and the amazing life of an idea* (Advanced Reader Copy ed.). New York, NY: Little, Brown and Company.

Reeves, D. (2021). *Deep change leadership: A model for renewing and strengthening schools and districts (a resource for effective school leadership and change efforts).* Bloomington, IN: Solution Tree Press.

Ritchie, S., & Bates, T. (2013). Enduring links from childhood math- ematics and reading achievement to adult socioeconomic status. *Psychological Science, 24*(7).

Rosenthal, A. K., & Lichtenheld, T. (2009). *Yes day!* (Illustrated ed.). HarperCollins.

Sackstein, S. (2021). *Assessing with respect: Everyday practices that meet students' social and emotional needs.* Alexandria, VA: ASCD.

Sackstein, S., & Hamilton, C. (2016). *Hacking homework: 10 strate- gies that inspire learning outside the classroom.* Cleveland, OH: X10 Publications.

Sandberg-Diment, E. (December 8, 1985). The executive computer. *TimesMachine.* Retrieved March 31, 2022, from https://time smachine.nytimes.com/timesmachine/1985/12/08/206974.html? pageNumber=278

Schwantes, M. (2019, October 5). *Steve Jobs: "Technology is nothing"—here's what he said it really takes to achieve great success.* CNBC, Make It. Retrieved from https://www.cnbc.com/2019/10/05/apple-ceo-steve-jobs-technology-is-nothing-heres-what-it-takes-to-achieve-great-success.html

Serrat, O. (2017). *The five whys technique.* Springer, Singapore. 10.1007/978-981-10-0983-9_32

Servitude, P. (2019, May 10). Public servitude. *Urban Dictionary.* Retrieved March 19, 2022, from https://www.urbandictionary.com/author.php?author=Public+Servitude

Sin, B. (2017). *These are the people who thought the iPhone would fail.* Retrieved from https://www.forbes.com/sites/bensin/2017/01/09/these-are-the-people-who-thought-the-iphone-would-fail/?sh=13f48169544e

Sinek, S. (2014). *Leaders eat last: Why some teams pull together and others don't.* New York, NY: Penguin Group LLC.

Smylie, M., & Murphy, J. (2021). *Caring in crisis: Stories to inspire and guide school leaders.* Thousand Oaks, CA: Corwin.

Sternin, J., & Choo, R. (2000). The power of positive deviancy. *Harvard Business Review.* Retrieved from https://hbr.org/2000/01/the-power-of-positive-deviancy

Sullivan, D., & Hardy, B. (2020). *Who not how.* Carlsbad, CA: Hay House.

Sun, T. (2009). *The art of war.* New York, NY: Penguin Group.

Sutherland, R. (2019). *Alchemy: The dark art and curious science of creating magic in brands, business, and life.* New York, NY: Haper Collins.

Suzuki, S. (2010). *Zen mind, beginner's mind.* Boulder, CO: Shambhala Publications.

The Speed Project. (2021). *Block starts: A guide to how they should be performed.* Retrieved from https://www.thespeedproject.com/sprinting/block-starts/

Thomas, A. (2021). Shipment forecast of tablets, laptops and desktop PCs worldwide from 2010 to 2024 (in million units). *Statista.* https://www.statista.com/statistics/272595/global-shipments-forecast-for-tablets-laptops-and-desktop-pcs/. Accessed 13 June 2021.

Tolstoy, L. (1993). *War and peace* (L. Maude & A. Maude, Trans.). Hertfordshire: Wordsworth Editions.

Trautwein, U., & Köller, O. (2003). The relationship between homework and achievement—still much of a mystery. *Educational Psychology Review*, 15, 115-145.

Trundley, R. (2018). *Changing lives and providing equity through pre-teaching and assigning competence.* Association of Teachers of Mathematics.

United States Government Accountability Office. (2016). *Better use of information could help agencies identify disparities and address racial discrimination.* Retrieved from https://www.gao.gov/assets/gao-16-345.pdf

U.S. Bureau of Labor Statistics. "Table 5. Number of private sector establishments by age." Retrieved December 12, 2021, from https://www.bls.gov/bdm/us_age_naics_00_table7.txt.

U.S. Bureau of Labor Statistics. "Business Employment Dynamics." Retrieved December 12, 2021, from https://www.bls.gov/bdm/entrepreneurship/entrepreneurship.htm.

Wahlstrom, K. L. (2014). *Examining the impact of later high school start times on the health and academic performance of high school students: A multi-site study.* Retrieved from https://conservancy.umn.edu/bitstream/handle/11299/162769/Impact%20of%20Later%20Start%20Time%20Final%20Report.pdf?sequence=1&isAllowed=y

Waitley, D. (1984). *The psychology of winning: Ten qualities of a total winner.* New York, NY: Berkley Book.

Weick, K. (1995). *Sensemaking in organizations.* Thousand Oaks, CA: Sage Publications.

Weller, C. (2017, September 4). Schools around the US are finally pushing back their start times—and it's working. *Business Insider.* Retrieved from https://www.businessinsider.com/school-start-times-are-finally-getting-pushed-back-2017-8

White, S. (2012, January 9). Time to think: Using restorative questions. *International Institute for Restorative Practices.* Retrieved April 2, 2022, from https://www.iirp.edu/news/time-to-think-using-restorative-questions

Whigham, N. (2016). The life changing inventions the experts said were impossible. *News.com.au.* Retrieved from https://www.news.com.au/technology/innovation/inventions/the-life-changing-inventions-the-experts-said-were-impossible/news-story/8c8b0e58532b329d1b6f97c3dfee9fcc

Willink, J. (2015). *Extreme ownership: How U.S. Navy SEALS lead and win.* New York, NY: St. Martin's Press.

Willink, J. (2020). *Leadership strategy and tactics: Field manual.* New York, NY: St. Martin's Publishing Group.

Wolfgang, L., & Striessnig, E. (2016). *Too educated to be happy? An investigation into the relationship between education and subjective well-being* [White Paper]. Federal Institute for Population Research. Retrieved from https://epc2016.princeton.edu/papers/160630

Woods. (2012). What is a data scientist?: Michael O'Connell of TIBCO spotfire. *Forbes*. Retrieved from https://www.forbes.com/sites/danwoods/2012/01/25/what-is-a-data-scientist-michael-oconnell-of-tibco-spotfire/?sh=37649719480a

Wujec, T. (2010, April). *Build a tower, build a team* [Video]. TED Conferences. Retrieved from https://www.youtube.com/watch?v=H0_yKBitO8M

Zabelina, D. L., & Robinson, M. D. (2010). Creativity as flexible cognitive control. *Psychology of Aesthetics, Creativity, and the Arts*, 4(3), 136-143. 10.1037/a0017379

INDEX

A SAGE Publishing Company

Helping educators make the greatest impact

CORWIN HAS ONE MISSION: to enhance education through intentional professional learning.

We build long-term relationships with our authors, educators, clients, and associations who partner with us to develop and continuously improve the best evidence-based practices that establish and support lifelong learning.